Selected Poems of VACHEL LINDSAY

selected poems of

VACHEL LINDSAY

edited by MARK HARRIS

THE MACMILLAN COMPANY, New York

COLLIER-MACMILLAN LIMITED, London

Fourth Printing 1966

The Macmillan Company, New York
Collier-Macmillan Canada, Ltd., Toronto, Ontario

Printed in the United States of America

Library of Congress catalog card number: 63–10660

Grateful acknowledgment is hereby made to the following copyright holders for permission to reprint copyrighted material:

To The Macmillan Company, Susan Lindsay, and Nicholas C. Lindsay for "The Chinese Nightingale," "The Raft," "Mark Twain and Joan of Arc," "How Samuel Bore Away the Gates of Gaza," "Niagara," "The Prairie Battlements," "The Broncho That Would Not Be Broken," "Our Mother Pocahontas," "The Merciful Hand," "Where Is the Real Non-Resistant?" and "The Ghost of the Buffaloes," from *The Chinese Nightingale and Other Poems*, copyright The Macmillan Company, 1917, renewed 1945 by Elizabeth C. Lindsay.

To The Macmillan Company, Susan Lindsay, and Nicholas C. Lindsay for "John L. Sullivan, the Strong Boy of Boston," "When the Mississippi Flowed in Indiana," "Daniel," "When Peter Jackson Preached in the Old Church," "After Reading the Sad Story of the Fall of Babylon," "The Springfield of the Far Future," "Alexander Campbell," "Bryan, Bryan, Bryan, Bryan," "The Statue of Old Andrew Jackson," "In Which

INTRODUCTION

In simple sheltered 1945, in quest of a girl to marry and a book to write, I discovered in Springfield, Illinois, not only the girl but also the poet Vachel Lindsay, married both, and have lived ever since in a polygamous awe arising from the repeated discovery that when I reach the truth of one or the other I am nevertheless as distant as ever: all roads lead not to finite horizons but merely to new turnings. I was twenty-three, if not too young to marry certainly too young to acknowledge any deficiency in myself likely to prevent me from promptly grasping every aspect of every motivation of a poet who was by that year fourteen years dead, whose geographical origin, educational training, and religious background were significantly different from my own, whose literary production was mature and extensive although my own had scarcely begun, and whose disposition, perhaps as the very result of that production, had led him to a despair I had not the least preparation to share. It was the year the bomb fell upon Hiroshima, a city in which I have since lived with my wife and the children of our Springfield union, and the year I undertook, with all the passion of a dedicated Know Nothing, a biography of the poet.

My passion was attacked but never subdued by the poet's sister, Olive Wakefield, of Springfield, her objections being that my mind was too young and unformed. These objections my young and unformed mind discounted as the peccadillo of a lady whose own mind had necessarily been weakened by long missionary years in China. My publisher, for different and less valid reasons, roughly ordered me to abandon the project, and I suffered, as a consequence, an affliction of spirit which settled in my lungs and left me almost dead in a Catholic hospital in Springfield. Luckily, I was rescued by nuns equipped with needles loaded with a new, war-born drug called penicillin, and by a devout lay nurse who in the moment of most extreme crisis actually restored warmth to my body by leaping upon me with her own; it was an act of mercy performed for my salvation in spite of the fact that my fevered tongue had continuously declared to her my contempt for her Church. Whether I was aware of it or not (these things take time) I was now better prepared than before—my mind less young, beginning to be formed—to seize hints of love, faith, charity, and hope.

Once more upon my feet, still far short of full strength or full understanding, I resumed my work. Over and over I read the books of Vachel Lindsay, traced his route through life upon calendars, index cards, and maps of the United States, accumulated mountains of correspondence, and visited persons who had known him in Springfield and elsewhere. It was my first excuse to place myself in the presence of men of artistic prominence—Louis Untermeyer and Langston Hughes in New York, Percy Grainger and John Sloan in New Mexico, and others, each of whom was indulgent, and all of whom warned me against haste.

For me, the most memorable of these interviews was with Edgar Lee Masters, who had already written a biography of Lindsay, and who was puzzled why anyone should attempt an improvement upon it. We met in the lobby of the Hotel Irving in New York on a fine autumn day. His face brightened as we shook hands, but he soon grew sullen and withdrawn, as one does who knows too much. He was well, but anxious to die. He stared briefly with wonder at an object nearly sixty years his junior, soon shifting his gaze to some memory upon the wall behind me, and the conversation proceeded, as his wife had warned me it would, principally between her and me. At the end of about twenty minutes she gently suggested that we had talked long enough. Masters agreed, and rose, adding only, "Vachel was the greatest of us all." It was the thought he meant me to carry away.

My book was subsequently published, not in haste, but perhaps too soon. On the other hand, how could I have put it off indefinitely? A writer must discharge his mistakes and go on to others; if they loom to embarrass him, so much the better: he can revisit them, as I am doing now, with the added advantage of having followed Lindsay upon the dangerous path of literary endeavor. On the day it was published I stood upon a street in Minneapolis, in the company of the poet Allen Tate, admiring my brilliant production in a bookshop window and trying to persuade Mr. Tate that if he would only read it (first buying it) he would learn what the life of a poet is like. Like Mrs. Wakefield before him, he appeared to be under the impression I was unready, and we passed on, he to the post office in flapping galoshes, and I into the future *via* Hiroshima.

I have carried about the world and down the years a great many books which, in one place or another, I have abandoned, but the shelf of Lindsay's books, and my own contribution to his history, have remained intact. In fancy and in fact they have altered. My interlinear and marginal notations in Lindsay's books, and in the Masters biography, have begun to fade, and my own volume, like some aged, wasting, distant cousin, occupies a sentimental place in the house without in the least contributing to the family's style, embarrassing us all with a shrill innocence very like the muttering of senility. Lindsay's work, on the other hand, has retained all the quality of energy, and has even ripened, newer and more moving passages apparently having flowered between those I formerly cherished, and whole poems inserted themselves. To be brief, it is simply astounding how the poetry of Vachel Lindsay has improved since 1945.

The life of Vachel Lindsay is so incredible in its details, and so rare an example of the extinct passion to mingle poetry with a programmatic national and religious purpose that we are compelled in the name of our own sane preservation to doubt that he actually lived it. We may comfort ourselves in recoil by charging that his effort was inspired by a vast illusion whose outcome could have been nothing less than his eventual despair. Thus we fortify ourselves with the conviction that he was the author of his downfall, and we relieve ourselves of the obligation to question whether the illusion was, in fact, illusion; or whether, even if it was, it was not the best of all illusions, especially for a poet.

Lindsay was born in Springfield in 1879, in a setting of family, house, neighborhood, city, and region not extraordinary except when endowed, as he would endow it, with properties of magical significance, investing its past with spiritual intentions inaccessible to orthodox historians, its present with a wondrous interior invisible to almost every eye but his own, and its future with a golden redemption of love and peace. His exuberance of faith was largely the gift of his mother, who introduced him early to time and space through books and art —"destined me, from the beginning, to be an artist . . . I am practically the person she made of me when I was eight." She transmitted to him both religious zeal and civic sense, eventually to become so well assimilated within him that the creation of his poetry would become his votive act, its sheer physical distribution a crusade not less arduous than the sacrifices of his missionary sister, and his final commitment to its necessity the agent of his mortal exhaustion. He was the second of six children—three of whom died in infancy—and the only son.

His father was a physician, the "Doctor Mohawk" of the poem. At Lindsay's birth the Springfield newspaper gratuitously promised him his father's practice, and the poet did for a time make motions as if in preparation for a medical career. Masters speculates that Lindsay "shrank from the . . . robustious tempo" of his father, adding that "the poet was in search of the soul of the U.S.A. . . . and with this adventure the doctor was evidently out of sympathy as something highly visionary. . . ."

This house divided into which Lindsay was born (in a downstairs bedroom; he died in the bedroom immediately above) had indeed once been owned by a sister-in-law of Abraham Lincoln. It stands to the present within a few blocks of Lincoln's home, both structures enshrined by decrees which invariably call up—at least into *my* mind—the cynical reflection that a municipality loves its best men best when they are inoffensively dead. Of his own family division Lindsay wrote:

My father had filled me with the notion that, way down in Kentucky, once upon a time a certain Abraham Lincoln came, with many soldiers. According to this tale they stole all the horses from my Grandfather Lindsay's estate, drove off all the negroes forever (my grandfather's personal property and mine), burned the crops, and then, in a way not mentioned, stole the farm, and left us all to begin again by studying medicine by a solitary candle. . . . This general view of history was challenged by my mother, who, though having many Southern ideas, was all for Lincoln. And I have in many ways agreed with her, but not enough to alter the fact that Mason and Dixon's line runs straight through our house in Springfield still, and straight through my heart.

House and heart divided, so was the city, for Springfield, Illinois, is only human after all, its avenues named for heroes but thronged with cowards, its best visions blasted, its police horrified. An elaborate and well-publicized celebration of the centennial of Lincoln's birth followed by less than a year a bloody race riot on the same streets, during which several lynchings occurred, one of them in the playground of the Edwards School. Nor does division end in Illinois.

A man's response to the divisions of the world—black, white, East, West, city, country, rose, lotus—tells us whether his illusion is of hope or of chaos. If he is a poet his illusion determines the tone and attack of the poems he will write, and it shapes his attitude toward his central metaphors. Since, for Lindsay, Springfield was central, the beginning and the end of his world, his America, his Babylon, his torment and his Heaven, we may define his illusion by examining the poem he dedicated "with great respect" to Masters. It begins:

> Here upon the prairie
> Is our ancestral hall.
> Agate is the dome,
> Cornelian the wall.
> Ghouls are in the cellar,
> But fays upon the stairs. . . .

To this, Masters' prevailing reply was that ghouls are also on the stairs, and coming up fast all through the house, and spilling onto the sidewalk and down the street, that they are in all the public buildings and on all the ships at sea, in the offices of all publishers and newspapers, that they control all industry and command the armies and the navies. Mysteries of heritage and temperament persuaded Vachel Lindsay that man was otherwise, Jeffersonian, basically good and ultimately perfectible: all the tragic divisions are reconcilable.

For one who was inclined to receive it, the political climate of Illinois encouraged optimism. The years of Lindsay's boyhood were also the years of agrarian and populist ferment, when it appeared that the small city, the town, the village, and the farm might still unite to prevent America's irreversible commitment to a machine economy and an urban culture. For a boy whose ancestral home lay within the shadow of the Illinois Statehouse, the era thrillingly permitted the simpler, idealistic instinct to join itself to political forces composed not only of disgruntled farmers but also of various degrees of sophisticated socialism. Populism was much more than (as Willard Thorp describes it in *The Encyclopaedia Britannica*) "cults and causes" ranged behind Bryan and Altgeld. It was a political and spiritual struggle waged for at least two decades against fate, history, and the tyranny of centralized capital, and it exerts to this day, although scattered and anonymous, an essential restraint upon every national program claiming a mandate.

It provided Lindsay with political heroes whose merely fleshly limitations he often sacrificed to his metaphor: where his heroes became involved his illusion was likewise involved. Grant him his sacred Springfield, grant him the right to call it the world, grant him the right to isolate fays from ghouls and believe in fays triumphant, and we must also grant him the right to populate his world with men whose spiritual devotion dominated all petty purpose. Not to grant the poet his metaphor is not to believe in the possibility of poetry.

And we must grant him also himself. He did not see men whole, we say, but only in their purest moments, a gallery of heroes, a litany of inviolate seekers in whom, we complain, we cannot believe, finding them so divorced from their own humanity, and knowing, ourselves, so much of ourselves and of the motives of men, and so much of Freud and all that. But yet, unless we are vulgarly asserting that humanity has no range except the one *we* believe in we must at last grant Vachel Lindsay his men and his metaphor, entire, total, and complete, assuming that what he saw in men and cities he must indeed have seen, because that was what was in *himself*, and why his life is incredible.

Between 1897, when he entered Hiram College, Ohio, ostensibly to study medicine and thus fulfill Springfield's blander expectations, and midsummer fifteen years later, Lindsay led a life so distinguished for apparent incompletion and quixotic and eccentric unsuccess that only our sturdiest belief in artistic process rescues our wavering faith. He afterward felt that "Springfield is . . . sure I should pretend to have been born 1912, and so ignore all my painful past." He attended college, studied art in Chicago and in New York, and in 1906, 1908, and 1912 embarked upon cross-country tramps. The sum of these flights and flounderings was his composition, in 1912, of *General William Booth Enters into Heaven*, whose publication in 1913 lifted him from obscurity. We must conclude that indolence may sometimes more properly be called meditation. These, then, were fifteen years of preparation.

At Hiram, where Lindsay remained three years and achieved the standing of a sophomore, he read widely but without clear objective in Shakespeare, Blake, Swinburne, Emerson, Lowell, Poe, Tennyson, and George Eliot, translating his reflections upon literature and other matters into journals whose introspection was designed to reveal how he might best serve Christ and mankind.

Now at thirty years of age Christ began his service of suffering. Up to that time he followed out his own individuality and his own environment for a complete knowledge and mastery of himself. It is for me to do otherwise. Let it be definitely understood that every inch of my will up to thirty-one years goes to the evolution of myself, and the perfection of the mental, physical, spiritual machine. Not till then am I to choose any great scheme of suffering, and self-spending. I have a world to save, and must prepare, prepare, prepare. . . . It behooves the Saxon to change his idea of heaven. Heaven is the New Earth it devolves upon the Saxon to establish. That must be his religion, his ideal, his ultimate heaven. . . . At last I am attending my choice of a college. It is organized within myself—the college of the love of the people. . . . When will the genius arise so strong that the strong shall fear him, so simple that the beast can understand him? Oh, the great poem has yet to be written. . . . It is well to undertake to be a certain limited self, a consecrated personality, to be supremely strong, and direct and gigantic and virile in the territory already staked out. I am strong and large and extensive enough now in outline. Let the rest of my life be simply doing my simple best. I write pretty well. I must write better. . . . Jeffersonian democracy as an art is a thing to be desired. Let us by all means be artistic democrats . . . Behold, I shall be a Caesar in the world of art, conquering every sort, every language and people, and lead their kings captive before the men of Rome. (Wow!)

From Hiram College he removed himself, in 1900, to Chicago, where he studied at the Art Institute, and in 1905 to The Chase School in New York. He hoped to earn his living as an illustrator. Meanwhile he was financially dependent upon his father, and upon gruesome odd jobs of the sort reserved for young men who have never been visionary enough to study double-entry bookkeeping. In Chicago he worked as a menial at Marshall Field's, at one point resolving to hold the job "for 2 or 3 years . . . by being extra useful," but in fact he remained only three months—in the toy department, an event insanely linked in my mind since 1945 with the lynching in the playground. He performed some sort of labor for a gas-tubing factory in New York, also for three months. These were his longest periods of steady employment. He was afterward to speak of the New York chapter of his life as "five years of grand free adventuring," but the trick of preserving himself within the framework of a senseless economic discipline must also have enforced his sense of identity with those outcasts who populate his poem *Booth*. Moreover, Lindsay would be Booth, too, outcast leader of the outcasts, who is rewarded by Christ in a "holy place" quite clearly the "court-house square" in Springfield, Illinois.[1]

Lindsay's failure as a pen-and-ink artist, aside from the question of "talent" viewed technically (as I am not prepared to view it), may be thought of in a different way: for "talent" finally resides in the artist's ability to find the truly suitable form for his feeling. Such a search requires time for error and false beginnings. At one point, in frustration or desperation or wild daring, Lindsay undertook to sell his work store-to-store to bakers, druggists, Italian confectioners, Negro cooks, fish-mongers, and Greek florists in midtown Manhattan; but these encounters, recorded in his journals, did not occur to him until afterward as the stuff of poems. When they did, as when *Booth* broke through for him, they became basic images to be wrought as rhythms for the ear, medleys of speech and event, informed by his classical awareness, and by his evangelical impulse, but set to the tune and tempo of American pace. We find him on Tenth Avenue:

The last laundry door I passed was unlocked. I said, By Jove I will land one of these heathen. I will capture the yellow man by his heartstrings. So I wandered to the desk. "Good evening, gentle-men," but the five swishing flat irons swung like gliding pendulums. . . . "I have here a beautiful and unworthy little poem for your exalted and celestial eyes." But the heathen kept on ironing. "Awake oh slumbering China, here is a message for you."

More than a decade later *The Chinese Nightingale* appeared. Its first lines are these:

"How, how," he said. "Friend Chang," I said,
"San Francisco sleeps as the dead—
Ended license, lust and play:

[1] Both Booth and Lindsay mingled religious zeal with the secular transaction. Booth, who founded the Salvation Army in England in 1878, outraged religious orthodoxy by carrying charity to the domestic poor, and by dispatching "missions" to the prisons and slums of London, often in defiance of the police. Author of *In Darkest England and the Way Out* (1890), he founded the periodical *War Cry*, whose title suggests Lindsay's *War Bulletin*, issued in Springfield during 1909. Lindsay had been sheltered at Salvation Army quarters in Atlanta in April, 1906, and in Newark in May, 1908.

Why do you iron the night away?
Your big clock speaks with a deadly sound,
With a tick and a wail till dawn comes round.
While the monster shadows glower and creep,
What can be better for man than sleep?"

"I will tell you a secret," Chang replied;
"My breast with vision is satisfied,
And I see green trees and fluttering wings,
And my deathless bird from Shanghai sings."

He had awarded the nameless Chinaman a name, moved him to San Francisco, and invested the heart with dreams. "Those that bought poetry under all disguises could not conceal from me that they had hearts full of dreams." He found himself, when peddling poems, in "a perfectly natural relation to society, as far as I am concerned. It is a situation in which I am much more at ease than peddling manuscripts or drawings from publisher to publisher."

On Wednesday, May 29, 1912, still without visible occupation or even prospects, and in his thirty-third year, Lindsay set out upon a new walking tour of the United States. It was to be his last in the style of "vain and foolish mendicant," and so racking that out of it must come either a surrender to practical arrangement, or renewed conviction. He was accompanied by a friend, George Lee, to the western limits of Springfield. Lee "told me good-by and gave me his blessing," and turned back. Lindsay, walking westward, followed the general route of the Santa Fe trail, a path worn by covered wagons and railroad and therefore somehow safe-sounding, but so awesome (even today, fifty years later) in its heat and pitiless solitude that its confrontation, "penniless and afoot," by a lone man armed only with a sheaf of prose and poetry, suggests a penultimate desperation. He walked to the Missouri line, across the breadth of Missouri, and into Kansas, which would soon provide him with current examples of that forlorn humanity whom General Booth succored, and with new, live images for other poems, notably *The Broncho That Would Not Be Broken.*

His "actual rules" of the road were "to have nothing to do with cities, railroads, money, baggage or fellow tramps. I was to begin to ask for dinner about a quarter of eleven and for supper, lodging and breakfast about a quarter of five. I was to be neat, truthful, civil and on the square." He slept, at best, in barns and livery stables, he harvested—mainly wheat—and he wrote letters home which were to become his fine prose volume, *Adventures While Preaching the Gospel of Beauty*. His position that "agricultural and middle west civilization" forms the best "natural America" may have been somewhat shaken by depressing views of racists, drunks, perverts, and whores of all colors; and perhaps he was shaken most of all by close inspection of the life of that kind of man—the itinerant harvester—who must have suggested to Lindsay a fore-featuring of his own dismal probabilities:

Stand with me at the station. Behold the trains rushing by, hour after hour, freight-cars and palace cars of dishevelled men! The more elegant the equipage the more do they put their feet on the seats. Behold a saturnalia of chewing tobacco and sunburn and hairy chests, disturbing the primness and crispness of the Santa Fe, jostling the tourist and his lovely daughter.

They are a happy-go-lucky set. They have the reverse of the tightwad's vices. The harvester, alas, is harvested. Gamblers lie in wait for him. The scarlet woman has her pit digged and ready. It is fun for the police to lock him up and fine him. No doubt he often deserves it. I sat half an afternoon in one of these towns and heard the local undertaker tell horrible stories of friendless field hands with no kinsfolk anywhere discoverable, sunstruck and buried in a day or so by the county. One man's story he told in great detail. The fellow had complained of a headache, and left the field. He fell dead by the roadside on the way to the house. He was face downward in an ant hill. He was eaten into an unrecognizable mass before they found him at sunset. The undertaker expatiated on how hard it was to embalm such folks.
. . .

The harvester is indeed harvested. He gambles with sunstroke, disease and damnation. In one way or another the money trickles from his loose fingers, and he drifts from the wheat in Oklahoma north to the wheat in Nebraska. He goes to Canada to shock wheat there as the season recedes, and then, perhaps, turns on his tracks and makes for Duluth, Minnesota, we will say. He takes up lumbering. Or he may make a circuit of the late fruit crops of Colorado and California. He is, pretty largely, so much crude, loose, ungoverned human strength, more useful than wise. Looked at closely, he may be the boy from the machine-shop, impatient for ready money, the farmer failure turned farm-hand, the bank-clerk or machine-shop mechanic tired of slow pay, or the college student on a lark, in more or less incognito. He may be the intermittent criminal, the gay-cat or the travelling religious crank, or the futile tract-distributer.[2]

From Kansas he walked as far as Wagon Mound, New Mexico, arriving September 12. He was more than a thousand miles from Springfield. Behind him and before him lay only desert. He telegraphed home for money, continuing then by train to Los Angeles where, at the home of an uncle, he wrote *General William Booth Enters into Heaven.*

The immediate occasion for the poem was Booth's death on August 20. But fifteen years of literary immersion preceded the dramatic moment, providing a center which Lindsay's imagination could supply and furnish out of monologue and bravado, out of a willful faith in a personal style, out of gospel hymns and secular broodings and wanderings to and fro.

Lindsay died a suicide in 1931, harvested. Done in. Had. He was fifty-two. My marginal notations for 1945 tell me exactly why—"society did it . . . look what society did to him!—" although I am now less inclined to press the case. In the end, every poet dies when his work is done, society his perennial exasperation, but never his killer. All poets are mad, or, to be gentler, estranged, alienated, perceiving too much, feeling too much, ranging too far, lingering too long at the poles of exaltation and morbidity. Not to explore life all the way is not to be a poet, and one must draw what consolation

[2] *Adventures While Preaching the Gospel of Beauty,* 158–160.

he can from the thought that the alternatives must be rather dull.

In Lindsay's case "success" took at first the happy form of ready publication. Thus his work is available to our solitude. It would have been well had he retained his own.

Unfortunately he was tempted—self-tempted—into a program of platform recitals, exhilarating at first, whose missionary character committed him beyond return. These tours, begun as a modest, noncommercial venture, were arranged by a college professor who soon found himself engaged in a crusade he had perhaps not envisioned. Lindsay's correspondence for this period maps campaigns of poets who will follow him, like Salvation Army platoons, like Johnny Appleseeds into the barren fields:

I certainly am willing [Lindsay wrote] to blast the breach in the wall, if you will send the 100 poets in my wake. . . . Say I am the least, the humblest and you have 99 stronger coming in behind me, and number 99, now hid in the womb of time is the foremost. And please tell the other poets . . . that I expect them to follow me up, and do a heap better than I do, that I do not claim a single thing for myself in the way of place or privilege. When I quit I want the 99 to be *well started, singing*.[3]

He felt himself "on the tantalizing verge of converting the *General Public*." In 1922 he declared that all America was "blocked in": within three years he would "do Australia, New Zealand and South Africa . . . the edges of the English speaking world."

We are planning not an economic, but an Art Revolution. . . . Once the Poets and Artists are in power, good-by to the business men, and tariff senators and such forevermore. We must make this a *Republic of Letters*.

Poetry was to be a liberating flame, the poet the runner with the torch. He recited, in time, to hundreds of thousands of people (perhaps, as he estimated, millions), carried through every State of the Union, and bearing by Pullman his gospel

[3] *Letters of Nicholas Vachel Lindsay*, ed. A. Joseph Armstrong, Baylor University Press: Waco, 1940.

of beauty for a nation presumably smoldering with esthetic desire. But by the time he apprehended his illusion the avenue of retreat was closed, escape had evaded him, the means had become the end. Such a mission necessarily involves its bow to gentility and public relations, dinner parties, fat ladies, sleepy men, and the crushing insult by which a man's face is mistaken for his work. It led Lindsay to a monumental contempt for precisely that social harmony he had been seeking all the days of his apprenticeship: his audiences never troubled themselves with his books, and by demanding that he recite night after night and city after city only those verses already famous they curdled even his own memories of his best labor.

His touring soon effectively displaced his writing as a way of life. As early as 1922 he complained, "how utterly impossible it has become for me to live a private life . . . I am like a newspaper or the front-door rug for everybody to use." He planned to say "good-by to all such schemes by July 1, 1923."

I see that for the most part my contact with the world *must be by deputy* . . . I *must* learn to live on a penny a day. *It is only on a penny a day that I can write.* I have hardly written a line for six years. I must learn to live on nothing and hide. It is the only way out for me. . . .

In November, 1924, he vowed, from Spokane, "I am here for all time so far as I know, and haven't the least notion of lecturing or traveling." But it was not to be. Seven years later he was still circling America on the railroad.

Why did he not retreat to his room in his house in Springfield? He had several times declared his wish to go home and draw. "I am sure I have pictures in me with as long fluid lines as the Congo, once I take a year or two to get the swing of it." Why was there no pausing?

Possibly he found unbearable the prospect of closeting himself for long creative periods bereft of the companionship of the optimism which had for a lifetime sustained him. In an age of carnage, the death of agrarian hope, the repudiation of Wilson, America's rejection of the League of Nations, the cynicism of Prohibition, the incoherence of Harding and

Coolidge, and the underlying vulgarity which these symptoms express, harbingers of hope must sound alarmingly detached from reality. That is to say that his work, then, was done.

I suppose no writer ever quite tells himself this, and I do not mean to say that Lindsay coldly knew it and therefore died. A fighting man fights on. There are at least a dozen writers now dashing about the United States whose significant work was long ago done, their fame made and their money spent, whose gracelessness depresses us all. Lindsay's symptoms of his late years, so strange and special to me in 1945, now appear to me the familiar, commonplace sorrows of writers to whom American society, in its shameless money lust, offers no climate for a second chance. His health waned. Writing of someone else, Lindsay observed: "He, like all promising Americans succeeded too quickly, and the limelight has done him no good." In search of an object for his wrath, Lindsay imagined himself betrayed by publishers, friends, and wife, all amalgamated in the hour of his death into an all-inclusive "they." He was full, to the end, of grandiose schemes for his own rejuvenation, suddenly empty, and plunged into so wretched a gloom that the account of his death, in Masters, must be read in installments. He carried his travail onto the public platform, committed rudenesses utterly alien to his former self, threatened violence, and wept in remorse.

He who had once marched with Booth on a dollar a day could not now live on ten thousand a year. Masters suggests that his situation could have been eased by the solitude a pension would have assured:

Springfield was then full of millionaires, not to mention Chicago, some of whom had made their money by exploiting and stealing the resources of the State; and others by operating mills of hate and false reports, ignorance, and calumny. They had thriven on the fame that Lindsay had brought to Illinois, while ignoring him, or libelling him. Money is all, practically and in the Marxian sense. Resolutions of respect, speeches, prayers, and even funeral wreaths are much cheaper than pensions, and make so much more noise!

So it may be. We are left to our speculations.

The poems included in the present volume are divided into sections, each section unified by theme in spite of the philosophical risk of declaring that a poem is "about" something; and, if so, what.

Basically they are the poems I happen to like best. Had anyone entrusted me with this task in 1945 my choices would have been different. I would have selected those poems which most directly address obvious social ills, for I began, of course, as Lindsay began, with the intention of doing nothing less than rehabilitating—absolutely reforming—a gross and greedy civilization. Young men who do not begin life in this way are despicable. But one learns, as one grows older, that a poem is a useful instrument of social reform only in proportion to its excellence *as poem.* "Art is pre-eminently didactic," Lindsay told his journal. "Artists always preach, if it is nothing more than their school of art."

These poems are a record of the illusion of Vachel Lindsay, which may well be the only possible illusion: are we not now absolutely compelled to resolve the divisions he defined, East, West, white, black, rose, lotus?

The City That Will Not Repent
May, 1961

CONTENTS

xxiii

Section Three 🐦
RUNES OF THE ROAD

Section Four 📙
POLITICS

Section Five 🌷
SONGS, PRAYERS, & SUPPLICATIONS
TO THE MUSE

xxvi

Section One

UNITED STATES
RHYTHMS

GENERAL WILLIAM BOOTH

ENTERS INTO HEAVEN

(To be sung to the tune of "The Blood of the Lamb" with indicated instrument)

1

(Bass drum beaten loudly.)
Booth led boldly with his big bass drum—
(Are you washed in the blood of the Lamb?)
The Saints smiled gravely and they said: "He's come."
(Are you washed in the blood of the Lamb?)
Walking lepers followed, rank on rank,
Lurching bravos from the ditches dank,
Drabs from the alleyways and drug fiends pale—
Minds still passion-ridden, soul-powers frail:—
Vermin-eaten saints with moldy breath,
Unwashed legions with the ways of Death—
(Are you washed in the blood of the Lamb?)

(Banjos.)
Every slum had sent its half-a-score
The round world over. (Booth had groaned for more.)
Every banner that the wide world flies
Bloomed with glory and transcendent dyes.
Big-voiced lasses made their banjos bang,
Tranced, fanatical they shrieked and sang:—
"Are you washed in the blood of the Lamb?"
Hallelujah! It was queer to see
Bull-necked convicts with that land make free.
Loons with trumpets blowed a blare, blare, blare
On, on upward thro' the golden air!
(Are you washed in the blood of the Lamb?)

II

(Bass drum slower and softer.)
Booth died blind and still by faith he trod,
Eyes still dazzled by the ways of God.
Booth led boldly, and he looked the chief
Eagle countenance in sharp relief,
Beard a-flying, air of high command
Unabated in that holy land.

(Sweet flute music.)
Jesus came from out the court-house door,
Stretched his hands above the passing poor.
Booth saw not, but led his queer ones there
Round and round the mighty court-house square.
Then, in an instant all that blear review
Marched on spotless, clad in raiment new.
The lame were straightened, withered limbs uncurled
And blind eyes opened on a new, sweet world.

(Bass drum louder.)
Drabs and vixens in a flash made whole!
Gone was the weasel-head, the snout, the jowl!
Sages and sibyls now, and athletes clean,
Rulers of empires, and of forests green!

*(Grand chorus of all instruments. Tambourines to the
foreground.)*
The hosts were sandalled, and their wings were fire!
(Are you washed in the blood of the Lamb?)
But their noise played havoc with the angel-choir.
(Are you washed in the blood of the Lamb?)
Oh, shout Salvation! It was good to see
Kings and Princes by the Lamb set free.
The banjos rattled and the tambourines
Jing-jing-jingled in the hands of Queens.

(Reverently sung, no instruments.)
And when Booth halted by the curb for prayer
He saw his Master thro' the flag-filled air.
Christ came gently with a robe and crown
For Booth the soldier, while the throng knelt down.
He saw King Jesus. They were face to face,
And he knelt a-weeping in that holy place.
Are you washed in the blood of the Lamb?

A Song in Chinese Tapestries

"How, how," he said. "Friend Chang," I said,
"San Franciso sleeps as the dead—
Ended license, lust and play:
Why do you iron the night away?
Your big clock speaks with a deadly sound,
With a tick and a wail till dawn comes round.
While the monster shadows glower and creep,
What can be better for man than sleep?"

"I will tell you a secret," Chang replied;
"My breast with vision is satisfied,
And I see green trees and fluttering wings,
And my deathless bird from Shanghai sings."
Then he lit five firecrackers in a pan.
"Pop, pop," said the firecrackers, "cra-cra-crack."
He lit a joss stick long and black.
Then the proud gray joss in the corner stirred;
On his wrist appeared a gray small bird,
And this was the song of the gray small bird:
"Where is the princess, loved forever,
Who made Chang first of the kings of men?"

And the joss in the corner stirred again;
And the carved dog, curled in his arms, awoke,
Barked forth a smoke-cloud that whirled and broke.
It piled in a maze round the ironing-place,
And there on the snowy table wide
Stood a Chinese lady of high degree,
With a scornful, witching, tea-rose face. . . .

Yet she put away all form and pride,
And laid her glimmering veil aside
With a childlike smile for Chang and for me.

The walls fell back, night was aflower,
The table gleamed in a moonlit bower,
While Chang, with a countenance carved of stone,
Ironed and ironed, all alone.
And thus she sang to the busy man Chang:
"Have you forgotten . . .
Deep in the ages, long, long ago,
I was your sweetheart, there on the sand—
Storm-worn beach of the Chinese land?
We sold our grain in the peacock town—
Built on the edge of the sea-sands brown—
Built on the edge of the sea-sands brown. . . .

When all the world was drinking blood
From the skulls of men and bulls
And all the world had swords and clubs of stone,
We drank our tea in China beneath the sacred spice-trees,
And heard the curled waves of the harbor moan.
And this gray bird, in Love's first spring,
With a bright-bronze breast and a bronze-brown wing,
Captured the world with his carolling.
Do you remember, ages after,
At last the world we were born to own?
You were the heir of the yellow throne—
The world was the field of the Chinese man
And we were the pride of the Sons of Han?
We copied deep books and we carved in jade,
And wove blue silks in the mulberry shade. . . ."
"I remember, I remember
That Spring came on forever,
That Spring came on forever,"
Said the Chinese nightingale.

My heart was filled with marvel and dream,
Though I saw the western street-lamps gleam,
Though dawn was bringing the western day,
Though Chang was a laundryman ironing away. . . .
Mingled there with the streets and alleys,
The railroad-yard and the clock-tower bright,
Demon clouds crossed ancient valleys;
Across wide lotus-ponds of light
I marked a giant firefly's flight.

And the lady, rosy-red,
Flourished her fan, her shimmering fan,
Stretched her hand toward Chang, and said:
"Do you remember,
Ages after,
Our palace of heart-red stone?
Do you remember
The little doll-faced children
With their lanterns full of moon-fire,
That came from all the empire
Honoring the throne?—
The loveliest fête and carnival
Our world had ever known?
The sages sat about us
With their heads bowed in their beards,
With proper meditation on the sight.
Confucius was not born;
We lived in those great days
Confucius later said were lived aright. . . .
And this gray bird, on that day of spring,
With a bright-bronze breast, and a bronze-brown wing,
Captured the world with his carolling.
Late at night his tune was spent.
Peasants,
Sages,
Children,
Homeward went,
And then the bronze bird sang for you and me.

We walked alone. Our hearts were high and free.
I had a silvery name, I had a silvery name,
I had a silvery name—do you remember
The name you cried beside the tumbling sea?"

Chang turned not to the lady slim—
He bent to his work, ironing away;
But she was arch, and knowing and glowing,
For the bird on his shoulder spoke for him.

"Darling . . . darling . . . darling . . . darling . . ."
Said the Chinese nightingale.

The great gray joss on the rustic shelf,
Rakish and shrewd, with his collar awry,
Sang impolitely, as though by himself,
Drowning with his bellowing the nightingale's cry:
"Back through a hundred, hundred years
Hear the waves as they climb the piers,
Hear the howl of the silver seas,
Hear the thunder.
Hear the gongs of holy China
How the waves and tunes combine
In a rhythmic clashing wonder,
Incantation old and fine:
    'Dragons, dragons, Chinese dragons,
    Red firecrackers, and green firecrackers
    And dragons, dragons, Chinese dragons.' "

Then the lady, rosy-red,
Turned to her lover Chang and said:
"Dare you forget that turquoise dawn
When we stood in our mist-hung velvet lawn,
And worked a spell this great joss taught
Till a God of the Dragons was charmed and caught?
From the flag high over our palace home
He flew to our feet in rainbow-foam—
A king of beauty and tempest and thunder

Panting to tear our sorrows asunder.
A dragon of fair adventure and wonder.
We mounted the back of that royal slave
With thoughts of desire that were noble and grave.
We swam down the shore to the dragon-mountains,
We whirled to the peaks and the fiery fountains.
To our secret ivory house we were borne.
We looked down the wonderful wing-filled regions
Where the dragons darted in glimmering legions.
Right by my breast the nightingale sang;
The old rhymes rang in the sunlit mist
That we this hour regain—
Song-fire for the brain.
When my hands and my hair and my feet you kissed,
When you cried for your heart's new pain,
What was my name in the dragon-mist,
In the rings of rainbowed rain?"

"Sorrow and love, glory and love,"
Said the Chinese nightingale.
"Sorrow and love, glory and love,"
Said the Chinese nightingale.

And now the joss broke in with his song:
"Dying ember, bird of Chang,
Soul of Chang, do you remember?—
Ere you returned to the shining harbor
There were pirates by ten thousand
Descended on the town
In vessels mountain-high and red and brown,
Moon-ships that climbed the storms and cut the skies.
On their prows were painted terrible bright eyes.
But I was then a wizard and a scholar and a priest;
I stood upon the sand;
With lifted hand I looked upon them
And sunk their vessels with my wizard eyes,
And the stately lacquer-gate made safe again.

Deep, deep below the bay, the seaweed and the spray,
Embalmed in amber every pirate lies,
Embalmed in amber every pirate lies."

Then this did the noble lady say:
"Bird, do you dream of our home-coming day
When you flew like a courier on before
From the dragon-peak to our palace-door,
And we drove the steed in your singing path—
The ramping dragon of laughter and wrath:
And found our city all aglow,
And knighted this joss that decked it so?
There were golden fishes in the purple river
And silver fishes and rainbow fishes.
There were golden junks in the laughing river,
And silver junks and rainbow junks:
There were golden lilies by the bay and river,
And silver lilies and tiger-lilies,
And tinkling wind-bells in the gardens of the town
By the black-lacquer gate
Where walked in state
The kind king Chang
And his sweetheart mate. . . .
With his flag-born dragon
And his crown of pearl . . . and . . . jade,
And his nightingale reigning in the mulberry shade,
And sailors and soldiers on the sea-sands brown,
And priests who bowed them down to your song—
By the city called Han, the peacock town,
By the city called Han, the nightingale town,
The nightingale town."

Then sang the bird, so strangely gay,
Fluttering, fluttering, ghostly and gray,
A vague, unravelling, final tune,
Like a long unwinding silk cocoon;
Sang as though for the soul of him

Who ironed away in that bower dim:—
    "I have forgotten
    Your dragons great,
      Merry and mad and friendly and bold.
Dim is your proud lost palace-gate.
I vaguely know
There were heroes of old,
Troubles more than the heart could hold,
There were wolves in the woods
Yet lambs in the fold,
Nests in the top of the almond tree. . . .
The evergreen tree . . . and the mulberry tree . . .
Life and hurry and joy forgotten,
Years on years I but half-remember . . .
Man is a torch, then ashes soon,
May and June, then dead December,
Dead December, then again June.
Who shall end my dream's confusion?
Life is a loom, weaving illusion . . .
I remember, I remember
There were ghostly veils and laces . . .
In the shadowy bowery places . . .
With lovers' ardent faces
Bending to one another,
Speaking each his part.
They infinitely echo
In the red cave of my heart.
'Sweetheart, sweetheart, sweetheart,'
They said to one another.
They spoke, I think, of perils past.
They spoke, I think, of peace at last.
One thing I remember:
Spring came on forever,
Spring came on forever,"
Said the Chinese nightingale.

☕ JOHN L. SULLIVAN,

THE STRONG BOY OF BOSTON

(Inscribed to Louis Untermeyer and Robert Frost)

When I was nine years old, in 1889,
I sent my love a lacy Valentine.
Suffering boys were dressed like Fauntleroys,
While Judge and Puck in giant humor vied.
The Gibson Girl came shining like a bride
To spoil the cult of Tennyson's Elaine.
Louisa Alcott was my gentle guide. . . .
Then . . .
I heard a battle trumpet sound.
Nigh New Orleans
Upon an emerald plain
John L. Sullivan
The strong boy
Of Boston
Fought seventy-five red rounds with Jake Kilrain.

In simple sheltered 1889
Nick Carter I would piously deride.
Over the Elsie Books I moped and sighed.
St. Nicholas Magazine was all my pride,
While coarser boys on cellar doors would slide.
The grown-ups bought refinement by the pound.
Rogers groups had not been told to hide.
E. P. Roe had just begun to wane.
Howells was rising, surely to attain!
The nation for a jamboree was gowned.—
Her hundredth year of roaring freedom crowned.
The British Lion ran and hid from Blaine
The razzle-dazzle hip-hurrah from Maine.

The mocking bird was singing in the lane. . . .
Yet . . .

To be sung.
Let the
audience join
in softly on
this tune,
wherever it
appears.

"East side, west side, all around the town
The tots sang: 'Ring a rosie—'
'London Bridge is falling down.' "
And . . .
John L. Sullivan
The strong boy
Of Boston
Broke every single rib of Jake Kilrain.

In dear provincial 1889,
Barnum's bears and tigers could astound.
Ingersoll was called a most vile hound,
And named with Satan, Judas, Thomas Paine!
Robert Elsmere riled the pious brain.
Phillips Brooks for heresy was fried.
Boston Brahmins patronized Mark Twain.
The baseball rules were changed. That was a gain.
Pop Anson was our darling, pet and pride.
Native sons in Irish votes were drowned.
Tammany once more escaped its chain.
Once more each raw saloon was raising Cain.
The mocking bird was singing in the lane. . . .
Yet . . .
"East side, west side, all around the town
The tots sang: 'Ring a rosie'
'London Bridge is falling down.' "
And . . .
John L. Sullivan
The strong boy
Of Boston
Finished the ring career of Jake Kilrain.

In mystic, ancient 1889,
Wilson with pure learning was allied.
Roosevelt gave forth a chirping sound.
Stanley found old Emin and his train.

Stout explorers sought the pole in vain.
To dream of flying proved a man insane.
The newly rich were bathing in champagne.
Van Bibber Davis, at a single bound
Displayed himself, and simpering glory found.
John J. Ingalls, like a lonely crane
Swore and swore, and stalked the Kansas plain.
The Cronin murder was the ages' stain.
Johnstown was flooded, and the whole world cried.
We heard not of Louvain nor of Lorraine,
Or a million heroes for their freedom slain.
Of Armageddon and the world's birth-pain—
The League of Nations, the new world allied,
With Wilson, crucified, then justified.
We *thought* the world would loaf and sprawl and mosey.
The gods of Yap and Swat were sweetly dozy.
We *thought* the far-off gods of Chow had died.
The mocking bird was singing in the lane. . . .
Yet . . .
"East side, west side, all around the town
The tots sang: 'Ring a rosie'
'LONDON BRIDGE IS FALLING DOWN.' "
And . . .
John L. Sullivan knocked out Jake Kilrain.

⏚ THREE POEMS ABOUT MARK TWAIN

I. The Raft

The whole world on a raft! A King is here,
The record of his grandeur but a smear.
Is it his deacon-beard, or old bald pate
That makes the band upon his whims to wait?
Loot and mud-honey have his soul defiled.
Quack, pig, and priest, he drives camp-meetings wild
Until they shower their pennies like spring rain
That he may preach upon the Spanish main.
What landlord, lawyer, voodoo-man has yet
A better native right to make men sweat?
This threadbare jester, neither wise nor good,
With melancholy bells upon his hood?

The hurrying great ones scorn his Raven's croak,
And well may mock his mystifying cloak
Inscribed with runes from tongues he has not read
To make the ignoramus turn his head.
The artificial glitter of his eyes
Has captured half-grown boys. They think him wise.
Some shallow player-folk esteem him deep,
Soothed by his steady wand's mesmeric sweep.

The little lacquered boxes in his hands
Somehow suggest old times and reverenced lands.
From them doll-monsters come, we know not how:
Puppets, with Cain's black rubric on the brow.
Some passing jugglers, smiling, now concede
That his best cabinet-work is made, indeed
By bleeding his right arm, day after day,

Triumphantly to seal and to inlay.
They praise his little act of shedding tears;
A trick, well learned, with patience, thro' the years.

I love him in this blatant, well-fed place.
Of all the faces, his the only face
Beautiful, tho' painted for the stage,
Lit up with song, then torn with cold, small rage,
Shames that are living, loves and hopes long dead,
Consuming pride, and hunger, real, for bread.

Here by the curb, ye Prophets thunder deep:
"What Nations sow, they must expect to reap,"

Or haste to clothe the race with truth and power,
With hymns and shouts increasing every hour.

The whole world on a raft! A Duke is here
At sight of whose lank jaw the muses leer.
Journeymen-printer, lamb with ferret eyes,
In life's skullduggery he takes the prize—
Yet stand at twilight wrapped in Hamlet dreams.
Into his eyes the Mississippi gleams.
The sandbar sings in moonlit veils of foam.
A candle shines from one lone cabin home.
The waves reflect it like a drunken star.

A banjo and a hymn are heard afar.
No solace on the lazy shore excels
The Duke's blue castle with its steamer-bells.
The floor is running water and the roof
The stars' brocade with cloudy warp and woof.

And on past sorghum fields the current swings.
To Christian Jim the Mississippi sings.
This prankish wave-swept barque has won its place.
A ship of jesting for the human race.

But do you laugh when Jim bows down forlorn
His babe, his deaf Elizabeth to mourn?
And do you laugh, when Jim, from Huck apart
Gropes through the rain and night with breaking heart?

But now that imp is here and we can smile
Jim's child and guardian this long-drawn while.
With knife and heavy gun, a hunter keen,
He stops for squirrel-meat in islands green.
The eternal gamin, sleeping half the day,
Then stripped and sleek, a river-fish at play.
And then well-dressed, ashore, he sees life spilt.
The river-bank is one bright crazy-quilt
Of patch-work dream, of wrath more red than lust,
Where long-haired feudist Hotspurs bite the dust . . .

This Huckleberry Finn is but the race,
America, still lovely in disgrace,
New childhood of the world, that blunders on
And wonders at the darkness and the dawn,
The poor damned human race, still unimpressed
With its damnation, all its gamin breast
Chorteling at dukes and kings with nigger Jim,
Then plotting for their fall, with jestings grim.

Behold a Republic
Where a river speaks to men
And cries to those that love its ways,
Answering again
When in the heart's extravagance
The rascals bend to say
"O singing Mississippi
Shine, sing for us today."

But who is this in sweeping Oxford gown
Who steers the raft, or ambles up and down,
Or throws his gown aside, and there in white

Stands gleaming like a pillar of the night?
The lion of high courts, with hoary mane,
Fierce jester that this boyish court will gain—
Mark Twain!
The bad world's idol:
Old Mark Twain!

He takes his turn as watchman with the rest,
With secret transports to the stars addressed,
With nightlong broodings upon cosmic law,
With daylong laughter at this world so raw.

All praise to Emerson and Whitman, yet
The best they have to say, their sons forget.
But who can dodge this genius of the stream,
The Mississippi Valley's laughing dream?
He is the artery that finds the sea
In this the land of slaves, and boys still free.
He is the river, and they one and all
Sail on his breast, and to each other call.

Come let us disgrace ourselves,
Knock the stuffed gods from their shelves,
And cinders at the schoolhouse fling.
Come let us disgrace ourselves,
And live on a raft with gray Mark Twain
And Huck and Jim
And the Duke and the King.

II. *When the Mississippi Flowed in Indiana*

(Inscribed to Bruce Campbell, who read Tom Sawyer *with me in the old house)*

Beneath Time's roaring cannon
Many walls fall down.
But though the guns break every stone,

Level every town:—
Within our Grandma's old front hall
Some wonders flourish yet:—
The Pavement of Verona,
Where stands young Juliet,
The roof of Blue-beard's palace,
And Kubla Khan's wild ground,
The cave of young Aladdin,
Where the jewel-flowers were found,
And the garden of old Sparta
Where little Helen played,
The grotto of Miranda
That Prospero arrayed.
And the cave, by the Mississippi,
Where Becky Thatcher strayed.

On that Indiana stairway
Gleams Cinderella's shoe.
Upon that mighty mountainside
Walks Snow-white in the dew.
Upon that grassy hillside
Trips shining Nicolette:—
That stairway of remembrance
Time's cannon will not get—
That chattering slope of glory
Our little cousins made,
That hill by the Mississippi
Where Becky Thatcher strayed.

Spring beauties on that cliffside,
Love in the air,
While the soul's deep Mississippi
Sweeps on, forever fair.
And he who enters in the cave,
Nothing shall make afraid,
The cave by the Mississippi
Where Tom and Becky strayed.

III. Mark Twain and Joan of Arc

When Yankee soldiers reach the barricade
Then Joan of Arc gives each the accolade.

For she is there in armor clad, today,
All the young poets of the wide world say.

Which of our freemen did she greet the first,
Seeing him come against the fires accurst?

Mark Twain, our Chief with neither smile nor jest,
Leading to war our youngest and our best.

The Yankee to King Arthur's court returns.
The sacred flag of Joan above him burns.

For she has called his soul from out the tomb.
And where she stands, there he will stand till doom.

. . .

But I, I can but mourn, and mourn again
At bloodshed caused by angels, saints, and men.

☙ IN PRAISE OF JOHNNY APPLESEED*

(Born 1775; died 1847)

I. Over the Appalachian Barricade

To be read like old leaves on the elm tree of Time, Sifting soft winds with sentence and rhyme.

In the days of President Washington,
The glory of the nations,
Dust and ashes,
Snow and sleet,
And hay and oats and wheat,
Blew west,
Crossed the Appalachians,
Found the glades of rotting leaves, the soft deer-pastures,
The farms of the far-off future
In the forest.
Colts jumped the fence,
Snorting, ramping, snapping, sniffing,
With gastronomic calculations,
Crossed the Appalachians,
The east walls of our citadel,
And turned to gold-horned unicorns,
Feasting in the dim, volunteer farms of the forest.
Stripedest, kickingest kittens escaped,
Caterwauling "Yankee Doodle Dandy."
Renounced their poor relations,
Crossed the Appalachians,
And turned to tiny tigers
In the humorous forest.
Chickens escaped
From farmyard congregations,
Crossed the Appalachians,

---

* The best account of John Chapman's career, under the name "Johnny Appleseed," is to be found in *Harper's Monthly Magazine*, November, 1871.

And turned to amber trumpets
On the ramparts of our Hoosiers' nest and citadel,
Millennial heralds
Of the foggy mazy forest.
Pigs broke loose, scrambled west,
Scorned their loathsome stations,
Crossed the Appalachians,
Turned to roaming, foaming wild boars
Of the forest.
The smallest, blindest puppies toddled west
While their eyes were coming open,
And, with misty observations,
Crossed the Appalachians,
Barked, barked, barked
At the glow-worms and the marsh lights and the lightning-
    bugs,
And turned to ravening wolves
Of the forest.
Crazy parrots and canaries flew west,
Drunk on May-time revelations,
Crossed the Appalachians,
And turned to delirious, flower-dressed fairies
Of the lazy forest.
Haughtiest swans and peacocks swept west,
And, despite soft derivations,
Crossed the Appalachians,
And turned to blazing warrior souls
Of the forest,
Singing the ways
Of the Ancients of Days.
And the "Old Continentals
In their ragged regimentals,"
With bard's imaginations,
Crossed the Appalachians.
And
A boy
Blew west,
And with prayers and incantations,

And with "Yankee Doodle Dandy,"
Crossed the Appalachians,
And was "young John Chapman,"
Then
"Johnny Appleseed, Johnny Appleseed,"
Chief of the fastnesses, dappled and vast,
In a pack on his back,
In a deer-hide sack,
The beautiful orchards of the past,
The ghosts of all the forests and the groves—
In that pack on his back,
In that talisman sack,
To-morrow's peaches, pears, and cherries,
To-morrow's grapes and red raspberries,
Seeds and tree-souls, precious things,
Feathered with microscopic wings,
All the outdoors the child heart knows,
And the apple, green, red, and white,
Sun of his day and his night—
The apple allied to the thorn,
Child of the rose.
Porches untrod of forest houses
All before him, all day long,
"Yankee Doodle" his marching song;
And the evening breeze
Joined his psalms of praise
As he sang the ways
Of the Ancient of Days.
Leaving behind august Virginia,
Proud Massachusetts, and proud Maine,
Planting the trees that would march and train
On, in his name to the great Pacific,
Like Birnam wood to Dunsinane,
Johnny Appleseed swept on,
Every shackle gone,
Loving every sloshy brake,
Loving every skunk and snake,
Loving every leathery weed,

Johnny Appleseed, Johnny Appleseed,
Master and ruler of the unicorn-ramping forest,
The tiger-mewing forest,
The rooster-trumpeting, boar-foaming, wolf-ravening
     forest,
The spirit-haunted, fairy-enchanted forest,
Stupendous and endless,
Searching its perilous ways
In the name of the Ancient of Days.

II. *The Indians Worship Him, but He Hurries On*

Painted kings in the midst of the clearing
Heard him asking his friends the eagles
To guard each planted seed and seedling.
Then he was a god, to the red man's dreaming;
Then the chiefs brought treasures grotesque and fair,—
Magical trinkets and pipes and guns,
Beads and furs from their medicine-lair,—
Stuck holy feathers in his hair.
Hailed him with austere delight.
The orchard god was their guest through the night.

While the late snow blew from bleak Lake Erie,
Scourging rock and river and reed,
All night long they made great medicine
For Jonathan Chapman,
Johnny Appleseed,
Johnny Appleseed;
And as though his heart were a wind-blown wheat-sheaf,
As though his heart were a new built nest,
As though their heaven house were his breast,
In swept the snowbirds singing glory.
And I hear his bird heart beat its story,
Hear yet how the ghost of the forest shivers,
Hear yet the cry of the gray, old orchards,

Dim and decaying by the rivers,
And the timid wings of the bird-ghosts beating,
And the ghosts of the tom-toms beating, beating.

But he left their wigwams and their love.
By the hour of dawn he was proud and stark,
Kissed the Indian babes with a sigh,
Went forth to live on roots and bark,
Sleep in the trees, while the years howled by.
Calling the catamounts by name,
And buffalo bulls no hand could tame.
Slaying never a living creature,
Joining the birds in every game,
With the gorgeous turkey gobblers mocking,
With the lean-necked eagles boxing and shouting;
Sticking their feathers in his hair,—
Turkey feathers,
Eagle feathers,
Trading hearts with all beasts and weathers
He swept on, winged and wonder-crested,
Bare-armed, barefooted, and bare-breasted.

The maples, shedding their spinning seeds,
Called to his appleseeds in the ground,
Vast chestnut-trees, with their butterfly nations,
Called to his seeds without a sound.
And the chipmunk turned a "summerset."
And the foxes danced the Virginia reel;
Hawthorne and crab-thorn bent, rain-wet,
And dropped their flowers in his night-black hair;
And the soft fawns stopped for his perorations;
And his black eyes shone through the forest-gleam,
And he plunged young hands into new-turned earth,
And prayed dear orchard boughs into birth;
And he ran with the rabbit and slept with the stream,
And he ran with the rabbit and slept with the stream,
And he ran with the rabbit and slept with the stream,
And so for us he made great medicine,

And so for us he made great medicine,
And so for us he made great medicine.
In the days of President Washington.

III. Johnny Appleseed's Old Age

Long, long after,
When settlers put up beam and rafter,
They asked of the birds: "Who gave this fruit?
Who watched this fence till the seeds took root?
Who gave these boughs?" They asked the sky,
And there was no reply.
But the robin might have said,
"To the farthest West he has followed the sun,
His life and his empire just begun."
Self-scourged, like a monk, with a throne for wages,
Stripped, like the iron-souled Hindu sages,
Draped like a statue, in strings like a scarecrow,
His helmet-hat an old tin pan,
But worn in the love of the heart of man,
More sane than the helm of Tamerlane!
Hairy Ainu, wild man of Borneo, Robinson Crusoe
    —Johnny Appleseed!
And the robin might have said,
"Sowing, he goes to the far, new West,
With the apple, the sun of his burning breast—
The apple allied to the thorn,
Child of the rose."

*To be read
like faint
hoof-beats
of fawns
long gone
From re-
spectable
pasture, and
park and
lawn,
And heart-
beats of
fawns that
are coming
again
When the
forest, once
more, is the
master of
men.*

Washington buried in Virginia,
Jackson buried in Tennessee,
Young Lincoln, brooding in Illinois,
And Johnny Appleseed, priestly and free,
Knotted and gnarled, past seventy years,
Still planted on in the woods alone.
Ohio and young Indiana—
These were his wide altar-stone,

Where still he burnt out flesh and bone.
Twenty days ahead of the Indian, twenty years ahead of
    the white man,
At last the Indian overtook him, at last the Indian hurried
    past him;
At last the white man overtook him, at last the white man
    hurried past him;
At last his own trees overtook him, at last his own trees
    hurried past him.
Many cats were tame again,
Many ponies tame again,
Many pigs were tame again,
Many canaries tame again;
And the real frontier was his sunburnt breast.
From the fiery core of that apple, the earth,
Sprang apple-amaranths divine.
Love's orchards climbed to the heavens of the West.
And snowed the earthly sod with flowers.
Farm hands from the terraces of the blest
Danced on the mists with their ladies fine;
And Johnny Appleseed laughed with his dreams,
And swam once more the ice-cold streams.
And the doves of the spirit swept through the hours,
With doom-calls, love-calls, death-calls, dream-calls;
And Johnny Appleseed, all that year,
Lifted his hands to the farm-filled sky,
To the apple-harvesters busy on high;
And so once more his youth began,
And so for us he made great medicine—
Johnny Appleseed, medicine-man.
Then
The sun was their turned-up broken barrel,
Out of which their juicy apples rolled,
Down the repeated terraces,
Thumping across the gold,
An angel in each apple that touched the forest mold,
A ballot-box in each apple,
A state capital in each apple,

Great high schools, great colleges,
All America in each apple,
Each red, rich, round, and bouncing moon
That touched the forest mold.
Like scrolls and rolled-up flags of silk,
He saw the fruits unfold,
And all our expectations in one wild-flower written dream.
Confusion, and death-sweetness, and a thicket of crab-
        thorns!
Heart of a hundred midnights, heart of the merciful morns.
Heaven's boughs bent down with their alchemy,
Perfumed airs, and thoughts of wonder.
And the dew on the grass and his own cold tears
Were one in brooding mystery,
Though death's loud thunder came upon him,
Though death's loud thunder struck him down—
The boughs and the proud thoughts swept through the
        thunder,
Till he saw our wide nation, each State a flower,
Each petal a park for holy feet,
With wild fawns merry on every street,
With wild fawns merry on every street,
The vista of ten thousand years, flower-lighted and com-
        plete.

Hear the lazy weeds murmuring, bays and rivers whisper-
        ing,
From Michigan to Texas, California to Maine;
Listen to the eagles screaming, calling,
"Johnny Appleseed, Johnny Appleseed,"
There by the doors of old Fort Wayne

In the four-poster bed Johnny Appleseed built,
Autumn rains were the curtains, autumn leaves were the
        quilt.
He laid him down sweetly, and slept through the night,
Like a stone washed white,
There by the doors of old Fort Wayne.

THE SANTA FE TRAIL

A Humoresque

(I asked the old negro: "What is that bird that sings so well?" He answered: "That is the Rachel-Jane." "Hasn't it another name—lark, or thrush, or the like?" "No. Jus' Rachel-Jane.")

I. In Which a Racing Auto Comes from the East

To be sung delicately, to an improvised tune.

This is the order of the music of the morning:—
First, from the far East comes but a crooning.
The crooning turns to a sunrise singing.
Hark to the *calm*-horn, *balm*-horn, *psalm*-horn.
Hark to the *faint*-horn, *quaint*-horn, *saint*-horn. . . .

To be sung or read with great speed.

Hark to the *pace*-horn, *chase*-horn, *race*-horn.
And the holy veil of the dawn has gone.
Swiftly the brazen car comes on.
It burns in the East as the sunrise burns.
I see great flashes where the far trail turns.
Its eyes are lamps like the eyes of dragons.
It drinks gasoline from big red flagons.
Butting through the delicate mists of the morning,
It comes like lightning, goes past roaring.
It will hail all the windmills, taunting, ringing,
Dodge the cyclones,
Count the milestones,
On through the ranges the prairie dog tills—
Scooting past the cattle on the thousand hills. . . .

To be read or sung in a rolling bass, with some deliberation.

Ho for the tear-horn, scare-horn, dare-horn,
Ho for the *gay*-horn, *bark*-horn, *bay*-horn.
Ho for Kansas, land that restores us
When houses choke us, and great books bore us!

30

Sunrise Kansas, harvesters' Kansas,
A million men have found you before us.
A million men have found you before us.

II. In Which Many Autos Pass Westward

I want live things in their pride to remain.
I will not kill one grasshopper vain
Though he eats a hole in my shirt like a door.
I let him out, give him one chance more.
Perhaps, while he gnaws my hat in his whim,
Grasshopper lyrics occur to him.

In an even,
deliberate,
narrative
manner.

I am a tramp by the long trail's border,
Given to squalor, rags and disorder.
I nap and amble and yawn and look,
Write fool-thoughts in my grubby book,
Recite to the children, explore at my ease,
Work when I work, beg when I please,
Give crank-drawings, that make folks stare
To the half-grown boys in the sunset glare,
And get me a place to sleep in the hay
At the end of a live-and-let-live day.

I find in the stubble of the new-cut weeds
A whisper and a feasting, all one needs:
The whisper of the strawberries, white and red
Here where the new-cut weeds lie dead.

But I would not walk all alone till I die
Without some life-drunk horns going by.
And up round this apple-earth they come
Blasting the whispers of the morning dumb:—
Cars in a plain realistic row.
And fair dreams fade
When the raw horns blow.

On each snapping pennant
A big black name:—
The careering city
Whence each car came.
They tour from Memphis, Atlanta, Savannah,
Tallahassee and Texarkana.

*Like a train-
caller in a
Union Depot.*

They tour from St. Louis, Columbus, Manistee,
They tour from Peoria, Davenport, Kankakee.
Cars from Concord, Niagara, Boston,
Cars from Topeka, Emporia, and Austin.
Cars from Chicago, Hannibal, Cairo.
Cars from Alton, Oswego, Toledo.
Cars from Buffalo, Kokomo, Delphi,
Cars from Lodi, Carmi, Loami.
Ho for Kansas, land that restores us
When houses choke us, and great books bore us!
While I watch the highroad
And look at the sky,
While I watch the clouds in amazing grandeur
Roll their legions without rain
Over the blistering Kansas plain—
While I sit by the milestone
And watch the sky,
The United States
Goes by.

*To be given
very harshly,
with a
snapping ex-
plosiveness.*

Listen to the iron-horns, ripping, racking.
Listen to the quack-horns, slack and clacking.
Way down the road, trilling like a toad,
Here comes the *dice*-horn, here comes the *vice*-horn,
Here comes the *snarl*-horn, *brawl*-horn, *lewd*-horn,
Followed by the *prude*-horn, bleak and squeaking:—
(Some of them from Kansas, some of them from Kansas.)
Here comes the *hod*-horn, *plod*-horn, *sod*-horn,
Nevermore-to-*roam*-horn, *loam*-horn, *home*-horn.
(Some of them from Kansas, some of them from Kansas.)

Far away the Rachel-Jane
Not defeated by the horns
Sings amid a hedge of thorns:—
"Love and life,
Eternal youth—
Sweet, sweet, sweet, sweet,
Dew and glory,
Love and truth,
Sweet, sweet, sweet, sweet."

To be read or sung, well-nigh in a whisper.

WHILE SMOKE-BLACK FREIGHTS ON THE DOUBLE-TRACKED
    RAILROAD,
DRIVEN AS THOUGH BY THE FOUL FIEND'S OX-GOAD,
SCREAMING TO THE WEST COAST, SCREAMING TO THE EAST,
CARRY OFF A HARVEST, BRING BACK A FEAST,
AND HARVESTING MACHINERY AND HARNESS FOR THE BEAST,
THE HAND-CARS WHIZ, AND RATTLE ON THE RAILS,
THE SUNLIGHT FLASHES ON THE TIN DINNER-PAILS.

Louder and louder, faster and faster.

And then, in an instant, ye modern men,
Behold the procession once again,
The United States goes by!
Listen to the iron-horns, ripping, racking,
Listen to the *wise*-horn, desperate-to-*advise* horn,
Listen to the *fast*-horn, *kill*-horn, *blast*-horn. . . .

In a rolling bass, with increasing deliberation.

With a snapping explosiveness.

Far away the Rachel-Jane
Not defeated by the horns
Sings amid a hedge of thorns:—
Love and life,
Eternal youth,
Sweet, sweet, sweet, sweet,
Dew and glory,
Love and truth.
Sweet, sweet, sweet, sweet.

To be sung or read well-nigh in a whisper.

The mufflers open on a score of cars
With wonderful thunder,
CRACK, CRACK, CRACK,
CRACK-CRACK, CRACK-CRACK,
CRACK, CRACK, CRACK,

To be brawled in the beginning with a snapping explosiveness, ending in a languorous chant.

Listen to the gold-horn . . .
Old-horn . . .
Cold horn . . .
And all of the tunes, till the night comes down

*To be sung to
exactly the
same whis-
pered tune as
the first five
lines.*

On hay-stack, and ant-hill, and wind-bitten town.
Then far in the west, as in the beginning,
Dim in the distance, sweet in retreating,
Hark to the faint-horn, quaint-horn, saint-horn,
Hark to the calm-horn, balm-horn, psalm-horn. . . .

*This section
beginning
sonorously,
ending in a
languorous
whisper.*

They are hunting the goals that they understand:—
San-Francisco and the brown sea-sand.
My goal is the mystery the beggars win.
I am caught in the web the night-winds spin.
The edge of the wheat-ridge speaks to me.
I talk with the leaves of the mulberry tree.
And now I hear, as I sit all alone
In the dusk, by another big Santa-Fe stone,
The souls of the tall corn gathering round
And the gay little souls of the grass in the ground.
Listen to the tale the cottonwood tells.
Listen to the windmills, singing o'er the wells.
Listen to the whistling flutes without price
Of myriad prophets out of paradise.
Harken to the wonder
That the night-air carries. . . .
Listen . . . to . . . the . . . whisper . . .
Of . . . the . . . prairie . . . fairies

*To the same
whispered
tune as the
Rachel-Jane
song—but very
slowly.*

    Singing o'er the fairy plain:—
    "Sweet, sweet, sweet, sweet.
    Love and glory,
    Stars and rain,
    Sweet, sweet, sweet, sweet. . . ."

✦ THE KALLYOPE YELL

(To be given in the peculiar whispered manner of the University of Kansas "Jay-Hawk Yell")

I

Proud men
Eternally
Go about,
Slander me,
Call me the "Calliope,"
Sizz. . . .
Fizz. . . .

II

I am the Gutter Dream,
Tune-maker, born of steam,
Tooting joy, tooting hope.
I am the Kallyope,
Car called the Kallyope.
Willy willy willy wah HOO!
See the flags: snow-white tent,
See the bear and elephant,
See the monkey jump the rope,
Listen to the Kallyope, Kallyope, Kallyope!
Soul of the rhinoceros
And the hippopotamus
(Listen to the lion roar!)
Jaguar, cockatoot,
Loons, owls,
Hoot, Hoot.
Listen to the lion roar,
Listen to the lion roar,

Listen to the lion R-O-A-R!
Hear the leopard cry for gore,
Willy willy willy wah HOO!
Hail the bloody Indian band,
Hail, all hail the popcorn stand,
Hail to Barnum's picture there,
People's idol everywhere,
Whoop, whoop, whoop, WHOOP!
Music of the mob am I,
Circus day's tremendous cry:—
I am the Kallyope, Kallyope, Kallyope!
Hoot toot, hoot toot, hoot toot, hoot toot,
Willy willy willy wah HOO!
Sizz, fizz. . . .

III

Born of mobs, born of steam,
Listen to my golden dream,
Listen to my golden dream,
Listen to my G-O-L-D-E-N D-R-E-A-M!
Whoop whoop whoop whoop WHOOP!
I will blow the proud folk low,
Humanize the dour and slow,
I will shake the proud folk down,
(Listen to the lion roar!)
Popcorn crowds shall rule the town—
Willy willy willy wah HOO!
Steam shall work melodiously,
Brotherhood increase.
You'll see the world and all it holds
For fifty cents apiece.
Willy willy willy wah HOO!
Every day a circus day.

What?

Well, *almost* every day.
Nevermore the sweater's den,

Nevermore the prison pen.
Gone the war on land and sea
That aforetime troubled men.
Nations all in amity,
Happy in their plumes arrayed
In the long bright street parade.
Bands a-playing every day.

What?

Well, *almost* every day.
I am the Kallyope, Kallyope, Kallyope!
Willy willy willy wah HOO!
Hoot, toot, hoot, toot,
Whoop whoop whoop whoop,
Willy willy willy wah HOO!
Sizz, fizz. . . .

IV

Every soul
Resident
In the earth's one circus tent!
Every man a trapeze king
Then a pleased spectator there.
On the benches! In the ring!
While the neighbors gawk and stare
And the cheering rolls along.
Almost every day a race
When the merry starting gong
Rings, each chariot on the line,
Every driver fit and fine
With a steel-spring Roman grace.
Almost every day a dream,
Almost every day a dream.
Every girl,
Maid or wife,
Wild with music,
Eyes agleam

With that marvel called desire:
Actress, princess, fit for life,
Armed with honor like a knife,
Jumping thro' the hoops of fire.
(Listen to the lion roar!)
Making all the children shout
Clowns shall tumble all about,
Painted high and full of song
While the cheering rolls along,
Tho' they scream,
Tho' they rage,
Every beast in his cage,
Every beast in his den,
That aforetime troubled men.

V

I am the Kallyope, Kallyope, Kallyope,
Tooting hope, tooting hope, tooting hope, tooting hope;
Shaking window-pane and door
With a crashing cosmic tune,
With the war-cry of the spheres,
Rhythm of the roar of noon,
Rhythm of Niagara's roar,
Voicing planet, star and moon,
SHRIEKING of the better years.
Prophet-singers will arise,
Prophets coming after me,
Sing my song in softer guise
With more delicate surprise;
I am but the pioneer
Voice of the Democracy;
I am the gutter dream,
I am the golden dream,
Singing science, singing steam.
I will blow the proud folk down,
(Listen to the lion roar!)
I am the Kallyope, Kallyope, Kallyope,

Tooting hope, tooting hope, tooting hope, tooting hope,
Willy willy willy wah HOO!
Hoot, toot, hoot toot, hoot toot, toot toot,
Whoop whoop, whoop whoop,
Whoop whoop, whoop whoop,
Willy willy willy wah HOO!
Sizz. . . .
Fizz. . . .

♻ DANIEL

(Inscribed to Isadora Bennett Reed)

<table>
<tr>
<td>Beginning
with a strain
of "Dixie."</td>
<td>Darius the Mede was a king and a wonder.
His eye was proud, and his voice was thunder.
He kept bad lions in a monstous den.
He fed up the lions on Christian men.</td>
</tr>
<tr>
<td>With a touch
of "Alexan-
der's Ragtime
Band."</td>
<td>Daniel was the chief hired man of the land.
He stirred up the music in the palace band.
He whitewashed the cellar. He shovelled in the coal.
And Daniel kept a-praying:—"Lord save my soul."
Daniel kept a-praying:—"Lord save my soul."
Daniel kept a-praying:—"Lord save my soul."</td>
</tr>
</table>

Daniel was the butler, swagger and swell.
He ran up stairs. He answered the bell.
And *he* would let in whoever came a-calling:—
Saints so holy, scamps so appalling.
"Old man Ahab leaves his card.
Elisha and the bears are a-waiting in the yard.
Here comes Pharaoh and his snakes a-calling.
Here comes Cain and his wife a-calling.
Shadrach, Meshach and Abednego for tea.
Here comes Jonah and the whale,
And the *Sea!*
Here comes St. Peter and his fishing pole.
Here comes Judas and his silver a-calling.
Here comes old Beelzebub a-calling."
And Daniel kept a-praying:—"Lord save my soul."
Daniel kept a-praying:—"Lord save my soul."
Daniel kept a-praying:—"Lord save my soul."

His sweetheart and his mother were Christian and meek.
They washed and ironed for Darius every week.

One Thursday he met them at the door:—
Paid them as usual, but acted sore.

He said:—"Your Daniel is a dead little pigeon.
He's a good hard worker, but he talks religion."
And he showed them Daniel in the lions' cage.
Daniel standing quietly, the lions in a rage.
His good old mother cried:—
"Lord save him."
And Daniel's tender sweetheart cried:—
"Lord save him."

And she was a golden lily in the dew.
And she was as sweet as an apple on the tree,
And she was as fine as a melon in the corn-field,
Gliding and lovely as a ship on the sea,
Gliding and lovely as a ship on the sea.

This to be repeated three times, very softly and slowly.

And she prayed to the Lord:—
"Send Gabriel. Send Gabriel."

King Darius said to the lions:—
"Bite Daniel. Bite Daniel.
Bite him, Bite him. Bite him!"

Thus roared the lions:—
"We want Daniel, Daniel, Daniel,
We want Daniel, Daniel, Daniel."

Here the audience roars with the leader.

And Daniel did not frown,
Daniel did not cry.
He kept on looking at the sky.
And the Lord said to Gabriel:—
"Go chain the lions down,
Go chain the lions down.
Go chain the lions down.
Go chain the lions down."

The audience sings this with the leader, to the old Negro tune.

And *Gabriel* chained the lions,
And *Gabriel* chained the lions,
And *Gabriel* chained the lions,
And Daniel got out of the den,
And Daniel got out of the den,
And Daniel got out of the den.
And Darius said:—"You're a Christian child,"
Darius said:—"You're a Christian child,"
Darius said:—"You're a Christian child,"
And gave him his job again,
And gave him his job again,
And gave him his job again.

✆ HOW SAMSON BORE AWAY
THE GATES OF GAZA

A Negro Sermon

Once, in a night as black as ink,
She drove him out when he would not drink.
Round the house there were men in wait
Asleep in rows by the Gaza gate.
But the Holy Spirit was in this man.
Like a gentle wind he crept and ran.
("It is midnight," said the big town clock.)

He lifted the gates up, post and lock.
The hole in the wall was high and wide
When he bore away old Gaza's pride
Into the deep of the night:—
The bold Jack Johnson Israelite,—
Samson—
The Judge,
The Nazarite.

The air was black, like the smoke of a dragon.
Samson's heart was as big as a wagon.
He sang like a shining golden fountain.
He sweated up to the top of the mountain.
He threw down the gates with a noise like judgment.
And the quails all ran with the big arousement.

But he wept—"I must not love tough queens,
And spend on them my hard earned means.
I told that girl I would drink no more.
Therefore she drove me from her door.
Oh sorrow!

43

Sorrow!
I cannot hide.
Oh Lord look down from your chariot side.
You made me Judge, and I am not wise.
I am weak as a sheep for all my size."

Let Samson
Be coming
Into your mind.

The moon shone out, the stars were gay.
He saw the foxes run and play.
He rent his garments, he rolled around
In deep repentance on the ground.

Then he felt a honey in his soul.
Grace abounding made him whole.
Then he saw the Lord in a chariot blue.
The gorgeous stallions whinnied and flew.
The iron wheels hummed an old hymn-tune
And crunched in thunder over the moon.
And Samson shouted to the sky:
"My Lord, my Lord is riding high."

Like a steed, he pawed the gates with his hoof.
He rattled the gates like rocks on the roof,
And danced in the night
On the mountain-top,
Danced in the deep of the night:
The Judge, the holy Nazarite,
Whom ropes and chains could never bind.

Let Samson
Be coming
Into your mind.

Whirling his arms, like a top he sped.
His long black hair flew round his head

Like an outstretched net of silky cord,
Like a wheel of the chariot of the Lord.

Let Samson
Be coming
Into your mind.

Samson saw the sun anew.
He left the gates in the grass and dew.
He went to a county-seat a-nigh.
Found a harlot proud and high:
Philistine that no man could tame—
Delilah was her lady-name.
Oh sorrow,
Sorrow,
She was too wise.
She cut off his hair,
She put out his eyes.

Let Samson
Be coming
Into your mind.

WHEN PETER JACKSON PREACHED
IN THE OLD CHURCH

(To be sung to the tune of the old negro spiritual "Every time I feel the spirit moving in my heart I'll pray")

Peter Jackson was a-preaching
And the house was still as snow.
He whispered of repentance
And the lights were dim and low
And were almost out
When he gave the first shout:
"Arise, arise,
Cry out your eyes."
And we mourned all our terrible sins away.
Clean, clean away.
Then we marched around, around,
And sang with a wonderful sound:—
"Every time I feel the spirit moving in my heart I'll pray.
Every time I feel the spirit moving in my heart I'll pray."
And we fell by the altar
And fell by the aisle,
And found our Savior
In just a little while,
We all found Jesus at the break of the day,
We all found Jesus at the break of the day.
Blessed Jesus,
Blessed Jesus.

⬧ THE CONGO

A Study of the Negro Race

(Being a memorial to Ray Eldred, a Disciple missionary of the Congo River)

I. Their Basic Savagery

Fat black bucks in a wine-barrel room,
Barrel-house kings, with feet unstable,
Sagged and reeled and pounded on the table,   *A deep rolling*
Pounded on the table,   *bass.*
Beat an empty barrel with the handle of a broom,
Hard as they were able,
Boom, boom, BOOM,
With a silk umbrella and the handle of a broom,
Boomlay, boomlay, boomlay, BOOM.
THEN I had religion, THEN I had a vision.
I could not turn from their revel in derision.
THEN I SAW THE CONGO, CREEPING THROUGH THE BLACK,   *More deliber-*
CUTTING THROUGH THE FOREST WITH A GOLDEN TRACK.   *ate. Solemnly*
Then along that riverbank   *chanted.*
A thousand miles
Tattooed cannibals danced in files;
Then I heard the boom of the blood-lust song
And a thigh-bone beating on a tin-pan gong.   *A rapidly*
And "BLOOD" screamed the whistles and the fifes of the   *piling climax*
    warriors,   *of speed and*
"BLOOD" screamed the skull-faced, lean witch-doctors,   *racket.*
"Whirl ye the deadly voo-doo rattle,
Harry the uplands,
Steal all the cattle,
Rattle-rattle, rattle-rattle,
Bing.
Boomlay, boomlay, boomlay, BOOM,"

With a philo-
sophic pause.

A roaring, epic, rag-time tune
From the mouth of the Congo
To the Mountains of the Moon.
Death is an Elephant,

Shrilly and
with a heavily
accented
metre.

Torch-eyed and horrible,
Foam-flanked and terrible.
Boom, steal the pygmies,
Boom, kill the Arabs,
Boom, kill the white men,
Hoo, Hoo, Hoo.

Like the wind
in the chim-
ney.

Listen to the yell of Leopold's ghost
Burning in Hell for his hand-maimed host.
Hear how the demons chuckle and yell
Cutting his hands off, down in Hell.
Listen to the creepy proclamation,
Blown through the lairs of the forest-nation,
Blown past the white-ants' hill of clay,
Blown past the marsh where the butterflies play:—
"Be careful what you do,

All the "o"
sounds very
golden. Heavy
accents very
heavy. Light
accents very
light. Last line
whispered.

Or Mumbo-Jumbo, God of the Congo,
And all of the other
Gods of the Congo,
Mumbo-Jumbo will hoo-doo you,
Mumbo-Jumbo will hoo-doo you,
Mumbo-Jumbo will hoo-doo you."

II. *Their Irrepressible High Spirits*

Rather shrill
and high.

Wild crap-shooters with a whoop and a call
Danced the juba in their gambling hall
And laughed fit to kill, and shook the town,
And guyed the policemen and laughed them down
With a boomlay, boomlay, boomlay, Boom.

Read exactly
as in first
section.

Then I saw the Congo, creeping through the black,
Cutting through the forest with a golden track.
A Negro fairyland swung into view,

48

A minstrel river
Where dreams come true.
The ebony palace soared on high
Through the blossoming trees to the evening sky.
The inlaid porches and casements shone
With gold and ivory and elephant-bone.
And the black crowd laughed till their sides were sore
At the baboon butler in the agate door,
And the well-known tunes of the parrot band
That trilled on the bushes of that magic land.

Lay emphasis on the delicate ideas. Keep as light-footed as possible.

A troupe of skull-faced witch-men came
Through the agate doorway in suits of flame,
Yea, long-tailed coats with a gold-leaf crust
And hats that were covered with diamond-dust.
And the crowd in the court gave a whoop and a call
And danced the juba from wall to wall.
But the witch-men suddenly stilled the throng
With a stern cold glare, and a stern old song:—
"Mumbo-Jumbo will hoo-doo you." . . .
Just then from the doorway, as fat as shotes,
Came the cake-walk princes in their long red coats,
Canes with a brilliant lacquer shine,
And tall silk hats that were red as wine.
And they pranced with their butterfly partners there,
Coal-black maidens with pearls in their hair,
Knee-skirts trimmed with the jassamine sweet,
And bells on their ankles and little black-feet.
And the couples railed at the chant and the frown
Of the witch-men lean, and laughed them down.
(Oh, rare was the revel, and well worth while
That made those glowering witch-men smile.)

With pomposity.

With a great deliberation and ghostliness.

With overwhelming assurance, good cheer, and pomp.

With growing speed and sharply marked dance-rhythm.

The cake-walk royalty then began
To walk for a cake that was tall as a man
To the tune of "Boomlay, boomlay, Boom,"
While the witch-men laughed, with a sinister air,
And sang with the scalawags prancing there:—

With a touch of negro dialect, and as rapidly as possible toward the end.

49

"Walk with care, walk with care,
Or Mumbo-Jumbo, God of the Congo,
And all of the other Gods of the Congo,
Mumbo-Jumbo will hoo-doo you.
Beware, beware, walk with care,
Boomlay, boomlay, boomlay, boom.
Boomlay, boomlay, boomlay, boom.
Boomlay, boomlay, boomlay, boom.
Boomlay, boomlay, boomlay,
Boom."

Slow philo-
sophic calm.

(Oh, rare was the revel, and well worth while
That made those glowering witch-men smile.)

III. The Hope of Their Religion

Heavy bass.
With a literal
imitation of
camp-meeting
racket, and
trance.

A good old Negro in the slums of the town
Preached at a sister for her velvet gown.
Howled at a brother for his low-down ways,
His prowling, guzzling, sneak-thief days.
Beat on the Bible till he wore it out
Starting the jubilee revival shout.
And some had visions, as they stood on chairs,
And sang of Jacob, and the golden stairs,
And they all repented, a thousand strong
From their stupor and savagery and sin and wrong
And slammed with their hymn books till they shook the
    room
With "glory, glory, glory,"
And "Boom, boom, Boom."

Exactly as in
the first
section.
Begin with
terror and
power, end
with joy.

Then I saw the Congo, creeping through the black,
Cutting through the jungle with a golden track.
And the gray sky opened like a new-rent veil
And showed the Apostles with their coats of mail.
In bright white steel they were seated round
And their fire-eyes watched where the Congo wound.
And the twelve Apostles, from their thrones on high
Thrilled all the forest with their heavenly cry:—

50

"Mumbo-Jumbo will die in the jungle;
Never again will he hoo-doo you,
Never again will he hoo-doo you."

Sung to the tune of "Hark, ten thousand harps and voices."

Then along that river, a thousand miles
The vine-snared trees fell down in files.
Pioneer angels cleared the way
For a Congo paradise, for babes at play,
For sacred capitals, for temples clean.
Gone were the skull-faced witch-men lean.
There, where the wild ghost-gods had wailed
A million boats of the angels sailed
With oars of silver, and prows of blue
And silken pennants that the sun shone through.
'Twas a land transfigured, 'twas a new creation.
Oh, a singing wind swept the negro nation
And on through the backwoods clearing flew:—
"Mumbo-Jumbo is dead in the jungle.
Never again will he hoo-doo you.
Never again will he hoo-doo you.

With growing deliberation and joy.

In a rather high key—as delicately as possible.

To the tune of "Hark, ten thousand harps and voices."

Redeemed were the forests, the beasts and the men,
And only the vulture dared again
By the far, lone mountains of the moon
To cry, in the silence, the Congo tune:—
Mumbo-Jumbo will hoo-doo you,
"Mumbo-Jumbo will hoo-doo you.
Mumbo . . . Jumbo . . . will . . . hoo-doo . . . you."

Dying down into a penetrating, terrified whisper.

This poem, particularly the third section, was suggested by an allusion in a sermon by my pastor, F. W. Burnham, to the heroic life and death of Ray Eldred. Eldred was a missionary of the Disciples of Christ who perished while swimming a treacherous branch of the Congo. See *A Master Builder on the Congo*, by Andrew F. Henesey, published by Fleming H. Revell.

☙ From "SO MUCH THE WORSE FOR BOSTON"

I read the aspens like a book, and every leaf was signed,
And I climbed above the aspen-grove to read what I could
    find
On Mount Clinton, Colorado, I met a mountain cat.
I will call him "Andrew Jackson," and I mean no harm by
    that.
He was growling, and devouring a terrific mountain-rat.
But when the feast was ended, the mountain-cat was kind,
And showed a pretty smile, and spoke his mind.
"I am dreaming of old Boston," he said, and wiped his jaws.
"I have often HEARD of Boston," and he folded in his
    paws.
"Boston, Massachusetts, a *mountain* bold and great.
I will tell you all about it, if you care to curl and wait.

"In the Boston of my beauty-sleep, when storm-flowers
    are in bloom,
When storm-lilies and storm-thistles and storm-roses are in
    bloom,
The faithful cats go creeping through the catnip-ferns,
And rainbows, *and* sunshine, *and* gloom,
And pounce upon the Boston Mice, that tremble under-
    neath the floors,
And pounce upon the big-eared rats, and drag them to the
    tomb.
For we are Tom-policemen, vigilant and sure.
We keep the Back Bay *ditches* and potato cellars pure.
Apples are not bitten into, cheese is let alone.
Sweet corn is left upon the cob, and the beef left on the
    bone.
Every Sunday morning, the Pilgrims give us codfish balls,

Because we keep the poisonous rats from the Boston halls."
And then I contradicted him, in a manner firm and flat.
"I have never seen, in the famous Hub, suppression of the
    rat."
"So much the worse for Boston," said the whiskery moun-
    tain-cat.

And the cat continued his great dream, closing one shrewd
    eye:
"The Tower-of-Babel Cactus blazes above the sky.
Fangs and sabers guard the buds and crimson fruits on high.
Yet cactus-eating eagles and black hawks hum through the
    air.
When the pigeons weep in Copley Square, look up, those
    wings are there,
Proud Yankee birds of prey, overshadowing the land,
Screaming to younger Yankees of the self-same brand,
Whose talk is like the American flag, snapping on the
    summit-pole,
Sky-rocket and star-spangled words, round sun-flower
    words, they use them whole.
There are no tailors in command, men seem like trees in
    honest leaves.
Their clothes are but their bark and hide, and sod and
    binding for their sheaves.
Men are as the shocks of corn, as natural as alfalfa fields.
And no one yields to purse or badge; only to sweating
    manhood yields,
To natural authority, to wisdom straight from the new sun.
Who is the bull-god of the herd? The strongest and the
    shaggiest one.
Or if they preen at all, they preen with Walter Raleigh's
    gracious pride:—
The forest-ranger! One grand show! With gun and spade
    slung at his side!
Up on the dizzy timber-line, arbiter of life and fate,
Where sacred frost shines all the year, and freezing bee and
    moss-flower mate."

☺ A RHYME ABOUT AN ELECTRICAL ADVERTISING SIGN

I look on the specious electrical light
Blatant, mechanical, crawling and white,
Wickedly red or malignantly green
Like the beads of a young Senegambian queen.
Showing, while millions of souls hurry on,
The virtues of collars, from sunset till dawn,
By dart or by tumble of whirl within whirl,
Starting new fads for the shame-weary girl,
By maggoty motions in sickening line
Proclaiming a hat or a soup or a wine,
While there far above the steep cliffs of the street

The stars sing a message elusive and sweet.
Now man cannot rest in his pleasure and toil
His clumsy contraptions of coil upon coil
Till the thing he invents, in its use and its range,
Leads on to the marvellous CHANGE BEYOND CHANGE.
Some day this old Broadway shall climb to the skies,
As a ribbon of cloud on a soul-wind shall rise.
And we shall be lifted, rejoicing by night,
Till we join with the planets who choir their delight.
The signs in the street and the signs in the skies
Shall make a new Zodiac, guiding the wise,
And Broadway make one with that marvellous stair
That is climbed by the rainbow-clad spirits of prayer.

⬥ NIAGARA

1

Within the town of Buffalo
Are prosy men with leaden eyes.
Like ants they worry to and fro
(Important men, in Buffalo).
But only twenty miles away
A deathless glory is at play:
Niagara, Niagara.

The women buy their lace and cry:—
"O such a delicate design,"
And over ostrich feathers sigh,
By counters there, in Buffalo.
The children haunt the trinket shops,
They buy false-faces, bells, and tops,
Forgetting great Niagara.

Within the town of Buffalo
Are stores with garnets, sapphires, pearls,
Rubies, emeralds aglow,—
Opal chains in Buffalo,
Cherished symbols of success.
They value not your rainbow dress:—
Niagara, Niagara.

The shaggy meaning of her name
This Buffalo, this recreant town,
Sharps and lawyers prune and tame;
Few pioneers in Buffalo;
Except young lovers flushed and fleet
And winds hallooing down the street:
"Niagara, Niagara."

The journalists are sick of ink:
Boy prodigals are lost in wine,
By night where white and red lights blink
The eyes of Death, in Buffalo.
And only twenty miles away
Are starlit rocks and healing spray:—
Niagara, Niagara.

Above the town a tiny bird,
A shining speck at sleepy dawn,
Forgets the ant-hill so absurd,
This self-important Buffalo.
Descending twenty miles away
He bathes his wings at break of day—
Niagara, Niagara.

II

What marching men of Buffalo
Flood the streets in rash crusade?
Fools-to-free-the-world, they go,
Primeval hearts from Buffalo.
Red cataracts of France today
Awake, three thousand miles away
An echo of Niagara,
The cataract Niagara.

Section Two

HOME TOWN

AFTER READING THE SAD STORY
OF THE FALL OF BABYLON

O Lady, my city, and new flower of the prairie
What have we to do with this long time ago?
O lady love,
Bud of tomorrow,
With eyes that hold the hundred years
Yet to ebb and flow,
And breasts that burn
With great-great-grandsons
All their valor, all their tears,
A century hence shall know,
What have we to do
With this long time ago?

KING ARTHUR'S MEN
HAVE COME AGAIN

(Written while a field-worker in the Anti-Saloon League of Illinois)

King Arthur's men have come again.
They challenge everywhere
The foes of Christ's Eternal Church.
Her incense crowns the air.
The heathen knighthood cower and curse
To hear the bugles ring,
But spears are set, the charge is on,
Wise Arthur shall be king!

And Cromwell's men have come again,
I meet them in the street.
Stern but in this—no way of thorns
Shall snare the children's feet.
The revelling foemen wreak but waste,
A sodden poisonous band.
Fierce Cromwell builds the flower-bright towns,
And a more sunlit land!

And Lincoln's men have come again.
Up from the South he flayed,
The grandsons of his foes arise
In his own cause arrayed.
They rise for freedom and clean laws,
High laws, that shall endure.
Our God establishes his arm
And makes the battle sure!

✣ DOCTOR MOHAWK

(Inscribed to Ridley Wills)

(A most informal chant, being a rhymed commentary on the preface, "Adventures While Singing These Songs,"* especially the reference to the Red Indian ancestor. To this he added a tradition that one branch of my mother's family came of the Don Ivans, of Spain.)

I. *Being a Seven-Year-Old Boy's Elaborate Memory of the Day of His Birth*

In through the window a sea-mustang brought me,
(Smashing the window sash, breaking the law).
I was tied to his back—I do not know who caught me.

Up from Biloxi, up the great Mississippi,
Through the swamps, through the thaw, through the rains
    that grew raw,
On the tenth of November (the hail storm was nippy).
Up the slow, muddy Sangamon River—
(While we heard the towns cough and we heard the farms
    shiver),
The high wave rolled on. We heard a crow squawk,
With a voice like a buzz saw, destroying the day:
"Caw, caw, you are rolling to meet the tall Mohawk,
He will burn you to ashes and turn you to clay,
He will burn like a scarecrow with fire in the straw,
You are rolling and whirling on to the Mohawk,
Caw, caw,
Caw, caw."

We sighted and broke the high hedge of Oak Ridge,
We rolled through its tombs. We saw Incubi walk.

The poem to be read with the greatest possible speed, imitating the galloping of a sea-mustang, each time faster till it is so memorized, all the reptends musically blended; almost as though the poem were one long word, then of course, read very slowly.

* *Collected Poems, 1930.*

We leaped the snow mounds like a pack of bloodhounds.
Dead lawyers were shrieking: *"You are breaking the law."*
We spoiled and howled down the shrill cemetery sounds,
Swept townward: a green wave, a foam wave, a moon
wave,
Up the dawn streets of Springfield, high tide in a cave,
Up to Edwards and Fifth street, and broke every window-
pane.
They thought we were "cyclone," earthquake, and rain.
We smashed the front door. We ramped by the bed's head.
On the wall-paper pattern sea-roses bloomed red.

There, for a ceiling bent crab-thorn, hazel-brush,
Red-haw, black-haw,
(And the storm blew a horn),
There fluttered a carrion crow that cried: *"Caw!"*
A scare-crow so queer, and a crow that cried: "Caw, *Caw!*
Caw!"

II. Being My Notion, as a Ferocious Small-Boy, of My Ancestral Protector

The porpoise was grandma. The Mohawk was doctor:
"Heap-big-chief-the-Mohawk," with eye like a tommy-
hawk.
Naked, in war-paint, tough stock and old stock,
Furious swash-buckler, street-brawler, world-breaker,
Plumed like an Indian, an American dragon,
Tall as Sun-Mountain, long as the Sangamon,
With a buffalo beard, all beast, yet all human,
Sire of the Mexican king, Montezuma,
Of Quetzal the Fair God, and prince Guatomozin,
And that fated Peruvian, Atahualpa,
Of King Powhatan and his brown Pocahontas,
And of everything Indian serious or humorous,
Sire of the "Mohocks" who swept through old London,

(Too dirty for Swift and too wicked for Addison);
He was carver of all the old Indian cigar-signs,
Chief of all the wild Kickapoo doctors,
And their log-cabin remedies known to our fathers,
Sire of St. Tammany, and sweet Hiawatha,
Tippecanoe, and Tyler Too,
He was named Joseph Smith, he was named Brigham
    Young,
He was named Susquehannah, he was named Mississippi,
Every river and State in the Indian Tongue,
Every park, every town that is still to be sung:—
Yosemite, Cheyenne, Niagara, Chicago!
The Pride of the U.S.A.:—*that* is the Mohawk,
The Blood of the U.S.A.:—*that* is the Mohawk,
He is tall as Sun-Mountain, long as the Sangamon,
Proud as Chicago, a dream like Chicago,
And I saw the wild Star-Spangled Banner unfurl
Above the tall Mohawk that no man can tame
Old son of the sun-fire, by many a name.

When nine, I would sing this yarn of the sea,
With ample embroidery I now must restrain
(Giving the facts and omitting the flowers)
It proved new fantastics were coming to me.
The Mohawk! the Mohawk! the Mohawk! the Mohawk!
Doctor and midwife! ancestral protector!
Breathed Mohawk fire *through* me, gave long claws *to* me,
Told my father and mother they must soon set me free,
Told the dears I had lived with a pearl in the billow
In the Mexican Gulf, in the depths of that sea,
For infinite years. Put the pearl by my pillow.
(It was new as that hour, and as old as the sea)—
The Soul of the U.S.A.—*that* was the pearl.
It became a white eagle I could not understand.
And I saw the carrion crow fly away.
And I saw the boughs open and the sun of that day,

63

And I saw the white eagle in the clouds fly and whirl
Then soar to the skies to a Star-Spangled Land.

And I cried, and held hard to my mother's warm hand.
And the Mohawk said:—"Red man, your first trial begins."
And the Mohawk roared:—"Shame to you, coward and
   mourner!"
And the Great Chief was gone.

But my life was all planned.

I wept with my mother. I kissed and caressed her.
Then she taught me to sing. Then she taught me to play:—
The sibyl, the strange one, the white witch of May.
Creating diversion with slow-talk and long-talk,
She sang with girl-pride of her Spanish ancestor,
The mighty Don Ivan, Quixotic explorer:—
Friend of Columbus, Queen Isabel's friend,
Conquistador!
Great-great-great-grandfather.

I would cry and pressed close to her, all through the story
For the Mohawk was gone. And gone was my glory:—
Though that white-witch adored me, and fingered each
   curl,
Though I saw the wild Star-Spangled Banner unfurl,
Though a Spanish Ancestor makes excellent talk.
I was a baby, with nothing to say
But:—"The Mohawk, the Mohawk, the Mohawk, the Mo-
   hawk."
And I knew for my pearl I must hunt this long way
Through deserts and dooms, and on till to-day.

I must see Time, the wild-cat, gorging his maw,
I must hear the death-cry of the deer he brought low,
And the cry of the blood on his pantherish paw,
And that carrion crow on his shoulder cry "Caw, Caw!
   Caw!"

III. One Brief Hour of Grown-up Glory on the Gulf of Mexico

Far from the age of my Spanish ancestor,
Don Ivan the dreamer,
Friend of Columbus, and Isabel's friend,
Wherever I wander, beggar or guest,
The soul of the U.S.A.:—that is my life-quest.

Still I see the wild Star-Spangled Banner unfurl.

And at last near Biloxi, in glory and sport
I met Doctor Mohawk, while swimming this morning
Straight into the Gulf of Mexico Sun.
The Mohawk! the Mohawk! the Mohawk! the Mohawk!
From the half-risen sun, in the pathway of blood.
Sea-roses swept round me, red-kissed of the flood.
And the flying fish whispered: "the First Trial is done."

Magnificent mischief now was a-borning.
First: I dived and brought up the cool dream called *"The
    Pearl."*
As far from the Mohawk as peace is from murder,
As far from the Mohawk as May from November,
As far from the Mohawk as love is from scorning,
As far from the Mohawk as snow is from fire.
Yet, the Mohawk arm lifted me out of that flood
(The blood of the U.S.A.—that is the Mohawk)
And he healed my sick heart where the thunder-winds hurl,
There in the fog, at the top of the sun
Cool were his foam-fins, majestic his graces,
Doctor, and glorious Ancestral Protector,
Exhorter, reprover, corrector.
Then we swam to the sky through crystalline spaces,
The clouds closed behind us, all the long way,
And a rainbow-storm priesthood that hour blessed the bay,
Medicine men, in tremendous array,

65

While he spoke to me kindly and yet with fine scorning
For hunting for favors with rabbits or men.
Breathed Mohawk fire through me, gave long claws to me
And told me to think of my birthday again:—
How the sun is a Mohawk, and our best ancestor:
I must run to him, climb to him, swim to him, fly to him,
And laugh like a sea-horse, or life will grow dim.
How only the Mohawks will call me their brother,
(We will flourish forever, breaking the law)
They are laughing through all of the lands and the oceans,
(And only great worlds make an Indian laugh)
They are singing and swimming their pranks and their
    notions
With poems, and splendid majestical motions,
And they will stand by me, and save and deliver,
With the pearl near my heart, they will love me forever,
An eagle, a girl, then a moon on the sand,
The bird of the U.S.A.—that is the darling—
Whirling and dancing, swimming with awe
In the light of the sun, in the infinite shining
Of the uncaptured future:—that is the darling.
The infinite future, that is the eagle,—
An eagle, a moon, a girl on the sand,
The Soul of the U.S.A.—that is the pearl,
Without flaw.

Note:—For the "Mohocks" read Gay's Trivia iii, 325; Spectator
Nos. 324, 332, 347; Defoe's Review, March 15, 1712; also Swift's
Journal to Stella.

✣ THE SOUL OF THE CITY RECEIVES
THE GIFT OF THE HOLY SPIRIT

(A broadside distributed in Springfield, Illinois)

Censers are swinging
Over the town;
Censers are swinging,
Look overhead!
Censers are swinging,
Heaven comes down.
City, dead city,
Awake from the dead!

Censers, tremendous,
Gleam overhead.
Wind-harps are ringing,
Wind-harps unseen—
Calling and calling:—
"Wake from the dead.
Rise, little city,
Shine like a queen."

Soldiers of Christ
For battle grow keen.
Heaven-sent winds
Haunt alley and lane.
Singing of life
In town-meadows green
After the toil
And battle and pain.

Incense is pouring
Like the spring rain

Down on the mob
That moil through the street.
Blessed are they
Who behold it and gain
Power made more mighty
Thro' every defeat.

Builders, toil on.
Make all complete.
Make Springfield wonderful.
Make her renown
Worthy this day,
Till, at God's feet,
Tranced, saved forever,
Waits the white town.

Censers are swinging
Over the town,
Censers gigantic!
Look overhead!
Hear the winds singing:—
"Heaven comes down.
City, dead city,
Awake from the dead."

❧ THE CORNFIELDS

The cornfields rise above mankind,
Lifting white torches to the blue,
Each season not ashamed to be
Magnificently decked for you.

What right have you to call them yours,
And in brute lust of riches burn
Without some radiant penance wrought,
Some beautiful, devout return?

*I recited these three poems more than any others in my
mendicant preaching tour through the West. Taken as a
triad, they hold in solution my theory of American civilization.*

I. The Proud Farmer

(In memory of E. S. Frazee, Rush County, Indiana)

Into the acres of the newborn state
He poured his strength, and plowed his ancient name,
And, when the traders followed him, he stood
Towering above their furtive souls and tame.

That brow without a stain, that fearless eye
Oft left the passing stranger wondering
To find such knighthood in the sprawling land,
To see a democrat well-nigh a king.

He lived with liberal hand, with guests from far,
With talk and joke and fellowship to spare,—
Watching the wide world's life from sun to sun,
Lining his walls with books from everywhere.

He read by night, he built his world by day.
The farm and house of God to him were one.
For forty years he preached and plowed and wrought—
A statesman in the fields, who bent to none.

His plowmen-neighbors were as lords to him.
His was an ironside, democratic pride.
He served a rigid Christ, but served him well—
And, for a lifetime, saved the countryside.

Here lie the dead, who gave the church their best
Under his fiery preaching of the word.
They sleep with him beneath the ragged grass . . .
The village withers, by his voice unstirred.

And tho' his tribe be scattered to the wind
From the Atlantic to the China Sea,
Yet do they think of that bright lamp he burned
Of family worth and proud integrity.

And many a sturdy grandchild hears his name
In reverence spoken, till he feels akin
To all the lion-eyed who build the world-
And lion-dreams begin to burn within.

II. *The Illinois Village*

O you who lose the art of hope,
Whose temples seem to shrine a lie,
Whose sidewalks are but stones of fear,
Who weep that Liberty must die,
Turn to the little prairie towns,
Your higher hope shall yet begin.
On every side awaits you there
Some gate where glory enters in.
Yet when I see the flocks of girls,
Watching the Sunday train go thro'
(As tho' the whole wide world went by)
With eyes that long to travel too,
I sigh, despite my soul made glad
By cloudy dresses and brown hair,
Sigh for the sweet life wrenched and torn
By thundering commerce, fierce and bare.
Nymphs of the wheat these girls should be:
Kings of the grove, their lovers, strong.
Why are they not inspired, aflame?
This beauty calls for valiant song—

For men to carve these fairy-forms
And faces in a fountain-frieze;
Dancers that own immortal hours;
Painters that work upon their knees;
Maids, lovers, friends, so deep in life,
So deep in love and poet's deeds,
The railroad is a thing disowned,
The city but a field of weeds.

Who can pass a village church
By night in these clean prairie lands
Without a touch of Spirit-power?
So white and fixed and cool it stands—
A thing from some strange fairy-town,
A pious amaranthine flower,
Unsullied by the winds, as pure
As jade or marble, wrought this hour:—
Rural in form, foursquare and plain,
And yet our sister, the new moon,
Makes it a praying wizard's dream.
The trees that watch at dusty noon
Breaking its sharpest lines, veil not
The whiteness it reflects from God,
Flashing like Spring on many an eye,
Making clean flesh, that once was clod.

Who can pass a district school
Without the hope that there may wait
Some baby-heart the books shall flame
With zeal to make his playmates great,
To make the whole wide village gleam
A strangely carved celestial gem,
Eternal in its beauty-light,
The Artist's town of Bethlehem!

III. On the Building of Springfield

Let not our town be large, remembering
That little Athens was the Muses' home,
That Oxford rules the heart of London still,
That Florence gave the Renaissance to Rome.

Record it for the grandson of your son—
A city is not builded in a day:
Our little town cannot complete her soul
Till countless generations pass away.

Now let each child be joined as to a church
To her perpetual hopes, each man ordained:
Let every street be made a reverent aisle
Where Music grows and Beauty is unchained.

Let Science and Machinery and Trade
Be slaves of her, and make her all in all,
Building against our blatant, restless time
An unseen, skilful, medieval wall.

Let every citizen be rich toward God.
Let Christ the beggar, teach divinity.
Let no man rule who holds his money dear.
Let this, our city, be our luxury.

We should build parks that students from afar
Would choose to starve in, rather than go home,
Fair little squares, with Phidian ornament,
Food for the spirit, milk and honeycomb.

Songs shall be sung by us in that good day,
Songs we have written, blood within the rhyme
Beating, as when Old England still was glad,—
The purple, rich Elizabethan time.

. . .

73

Say, is my prophecy too fair and far?
I only know, unless her faith be high,
The soul of this, our Nineveh, is doomed,
Our little Babylon will surely die.

Some city on the breast of Illinois
No wiser and no better at the start
By faith shall rise redeemed, by faith shall rise
Bearing the western glory in her heart.

The genius of the Maple, Elm and Oak,
The secret hidden in each grain of corn,
The glory that the prairie angels sing
At night when sons of Life and Love are born,

Born but to struggle, squalid and alone,
Broken and wandering in their early years.
When will they make our dusty streets their goal,
Within our attics hide their sacred tears?

When will they start our vulgar blood athrill
With living language, words that set us free?
When will they make a path of beauty clear
Between our riches and our liberty?

We must have many Lincoln-hearted men.
A city is not builded in a day.
And they must do their work, and come and go,
While countless generations pass away.

EPILOGUE TO THE ADVENTURES WHILE PREACHING THE GOSPEL OF BEAUTY

(Written to all young lovers about to set up homes of their own—but especially to those of some far-distant day, and those of my home-village.)

Lovers, O lovers, listen to my call.
    Give me kind thoughts. I woo you on my knees.
Lovers, pale lovers, when the wheat grows tall,
    When willow trees are Eden's incense trees:—

I would be welcome as the rose in flower
    Or busy bird in your most secret fane.
I would be read in your transcendent hour
    When book and rhyme seem for the most part vain.

I would be read, the while you kiss and pray.
    I would be read, ere the betrothal ring
Circles the slender finger and you say
    Words out of Heaven, while your pulses sing.

O lovers, be my partisans and build
    Each home with a great fireplace as is meet.
When there you stand, with royal wonder filled,
    In bridal peace, and comradeship complete,

While each dear heart beats like a fairy drum—
    Then burn a new-ripe wheat-sheaf in my name.
Out of the fire my spirit-bread shall come
    And my soul's gospel swirl from that red flame.

75

In this, the City of my Discontent,
Sometimes there comes a whisper from the grass,
"Romance, Romance—is here. No Hindu town
Is quite so strange. No Citadel of Brass
By Sinbad found, held half such love and hate;
No picture-palace in a picture-book
Such webs of Friendship, Beauty, Greed and Fate!"

In this, the City of my Discontent,
Down from the sky, up from the smoking deep
Wild legends new and old burn round my bed
While trees and grass and men are wrapped in sleep.
Angels come down, with Christmas in their hearts,
Gentle, whimsical, laughing, heaven-sent;
And, for a day, fair Peace have given me
In this, the City of my Discontent!

THE TOWN OF AMERICAN VISIONS

(Springfield, Illinois)

Is it for naught that where the tired crowds see
Only a place for trade, a teeming square,
Doors of high portent open unto me
Carved with great eagles, and with hawthorns rare?

Doors I proclaim, for there are rooms forgot
Ripened through æons by the good and wise:
Walls set with Art's own pearl and amethyst
Angel-wrought hangings there, and heaven-hued dyes:—

Dazzling the eye of faith, the hope-filled heart:
Rooms rich in records of old deeds sublime:
Books that hold garnered harvests of far lands,
Pictures that tableau Man's triumphant climb:

Statues so white, so counterfeiting life,
Bronze so ennobled, so with glory fraught
That the tired eyes must weep with joy to see
And the tired mind in Beauty's net be caught.

Come enter there, and meet Tomorrow's Man,
Communing with him softly day by day.
Ah, the deep vistas he reveals, the dream
Of angel-bands in infinite array—

Bright angel-bands, that dance in paths of earth
When our despairs are gone, long overpast—
When men and maidens give fair hearts to Christ
And white streets flame in righteous peace at last.

THE SPRINGFIELD
OF THE FAR FUTURE

Some day our town will grow old.
"She is wicked and raw," men say,
"Awkward and brash and profane."
But the years have a healing way.
The years of God are like bread,
Balm of Gilead and sweet.
And the soul of this little town
Our Father will make complete.

Some day our town will grow old,
Filled with the fullness of time,
Treasure on treasure heaped
Of beauty's tradition sublime.
Proud and gay and gray
Like Hannah with Samuel blest.
Humble and girlish and white
Like Mary, the manger guest.

Like Mary the manger queen
Bringing the God of Light
Till Christmas is here indeed
And earth has no more of night,
And hosts of Magi come,
The wisest under the sun
Bringing frankincense and praise
For her gift of the Infinite One.

"The present material universe, yet unrevealed in all its area, in all its tenantries, in all its riches, beauty and grandeur, will be wholly regenerated. Of this fact we have full assurance since He that now sits upon the throne of the Universe has pledged His word for it, saying: 'Behold I will create all things new,' consequently, 'new heavens, new earth,' consequently, new tenantries, new employments, new pleasures, new joys, new ecstasies. There is a fullness of joy, a fullness of glory, and a fullness of blessedness of which no living man however enlightened, however enlarged, however gifted, ever formed or entertained one adequate conception."

The above is the closing paragraph in Alexander Campbell's last essay in the *Millennial Harbinger*, which he had edited thirty-five years. This paragraph appeared November, 1865, four months before his death.

I. My Fathers Came from Kentucky

I was born in Illinois,—
Have lived there many days.
And I have Northern words,
And thoughts,
And ways.

But my great-grandfathers came
To the west with Daniel Boone,
And taught his babes to read,
And heard the redbird's tune;

And heard the turkey's call,
And stilled the panther's cry,
And rolled on the blue-grass hills,
And looked God in the eye.

And feud and Hell were theirs;
Love, like the moon's desire,
Love like a burning-mine,
Love like rifle-fire.

I tell tales out of school
Till these Yankees hate my style.
Why should the young cad cry,
Shout with joy for a mile?

Why do I faint with love
Till the prairies dip and reel?
My heart is a kicking horse
Shod with Kentucky steel.

No drop of my blood from north
Of Mason and Dixon's line.
And this racer in my breast
Tears my ribs for a sign.

But I ran in Kentucky hills
Last week. They were hearth and home.
And the church at Grassy Springs,
Under the redbird's wings
Was peace and honeycomb.

II. *Written in a Year When Many of My People Died*

I have begun to count my dead.
They wave green branches
Around my head,
Put their hands upon my shoulders,
Stand behind me,
Fly above me—
Presences that love me.
They watch me daily,

Murmuring, gravely, gaily,
Praising, reproving, readily.
And every year that company
Grows the greater steadily.
And every day I count my dead
In robes of sunrise, blue and red.

III. *A Rhymed Address to All Renegade Camp-bellites, Exhorting Them to Return*

I

O prodigal son, O recreant daughter,
When broken by the death of a child
You called for the graybeard Campbellite elder,
Who spoke as of old in the wild.
His voice held echoes of the deep woods of Kentucky.
He towered in apostolic state,
While the portrait of Campbell emerged from the dark:
That genius beautiful and great.
And millennial trumpets poised, half lifted,
Millennial trumpets that wait.

II

Like the woods of old Kentucky
The memories of childhood
Arch up to where gold chariot wheels go ringing,
To where the precious airs are terraces and roadways
For witnesses to God, forever singing.
Like Mammoth Cave, Kentucky, the memories of child-
hood
Go in and in forever underground
To river and fountain of whispering and mystery
And many a haunted hall without a sound.
To Indian hoards and carvings and graveyards unexplored.

To pits so deep a torch turns to a star
Whirling 'round and going down to the deepest rocks of
    earth,
To the fiery roots of forests brave and far.

III

As I built cob-houses with small cousins on the floor:
(The talk was not meant for me).
Daguerreotypes shone. The back log sizzled
And my grandmother traced the family tree.
Then she swept to the proverbs of Campbell again.
And we glanced at the portrait of that most benign of men
Looking down through the evening gleam
With a bit of Andrew Jackson's air,
More of Henry Clay
And the statesmen of Thomas Jefferson's day:
With the face of age,
And the flush of youth,
And that air of going on, forever free.

For once upon a time . . .
Long, long ago . . .
In the holy forest land
There was a jolly pre-millennial band,
When that text-armed apostle, Alexander Campbell
Held deathless debate with the wicked "infi-del."
The clearing was a picnic ground.
Squirrels were barking.
The seventeen-year locust charged by.
Wild turkeys perched on high.
And millions of wild pigeons
Broke the limbs of trees,
Then shut out the sun, as they swept on their way.
But ah, the wilder dove of God flew down
To bring a secret glory, and to stay,
With the proud hunter-trappers, patriarchs that came

To break bread together and to pray
And oh the music of each living throbbing thing
When Campbell arose,
A pillar of fire,
The great high priest of the Spring.

He stepped from out the Brush Run Meeting House
To make the big woods his cathedrals,
The river his baptismal font,
The rolling clouds his bells,
The storming skies his waterfalls,
His pastures and his wells.
Despite all sternness in his word
Richer grew the rushing blood
Within our fathers' coldest thought.
Imagination at the flood
Made flowery all they heard.
The deep communion cup
Of the whole South lifted up.

Who were the witnesses, the great cloud of witnesses
With which he was compassed around?
The heroes of faith from the days of Abraham
Stood on that blue-grass ground—
While the battle-ax of thought
Hewed to the bone
That the utmost generation
Till the world was set right
Might have an America their own.
For religion Dionysian
Was far from Campbell's doctrine.

He preached with faultless logic
An American Millennium:
The social order
Of a realist and farmer
With every neighbor
Within stone wall and border.

And the tongues of flame came down
Almost in spite of him.
And now all but that Pentecost is dim.

IV

I walk the forest by the Daniel Boone trail.
By guide posts quaint.
And the blazes are faint
In the rough old bark
Of silver poplars
And elms once slim,
Now monoliths tall.
I walk the aisle,
The cathedral hall
That is haunted still
With chariots dim,
Whispering still
With debate and call.

I come to you from Campbell,
Turn again, prodigal
Haunted by his name!
Artist, singer, builder,
The forest's son or daughter!
You, the blasphemer
Will yet know repentance,
And Campbell old and gray
Will lead you to the dream-side
Of a pennyroyal river.
While your proud heart is shaken
Your confession will be taken
And your sins baptized away.

You, statesman-philosopher,
Sage with high conceit
Who speak of revolutions, in long words,

And guide the little world as best you may:
I come to you from Campbell
And say he rides your way
And will wait with you the coming of his day.
His horse still threads the forest,
Though the storm be roaring down. . . .
Campbell enters now your log-house door.
Indeed you make him welcome, after many years,
While the children build cob-houses on the floor.

Let a thousand prophets have their due.
Let each have his boat in the sky.
But you were born for his secular millennium
With the old Kentucky forest blooming like Heaven,
And the redbirds flying high.

JOHNNY APPLESEED SPEAKS OF THE APPLE-BLOSSOM AMARANTH THAT WILL COME TO THIS CITY

Now, in the night, all music haunts us here . . .
Is it for nothing heaven cracks and yawns
And the tremendous amaranth descends,
Loaded with glory of ten thousand dawns?

The amaranth means:—God would have us say:—
"Whether you will or no, O city young,
Heaven will bloom like one great flower for you:
Flash and loom greatly, all your streets among."

Friend, I will not stop hoping, though you mourn.
We see such flowers, and some of them shall come,
Though now our streets are jazzed, or sadly gray,
And though our boys are strident now, or dumb.

Friend, that flower-town, that wonder town shall come,
Naught can prevent it. Though it may not be
What we may plan, it comes, at last—we know
With streets like channels of an incense sea,—

With twilight mists from heaven's jungles deep,
Or where the butterfly's great soul
    Still floats asleep—
    Beneath great heaven's granite steep;—
It comes, at last we know,
With musical bells, from the great western tree,
From the far star, or golden maids that come
From Eve's great eastern palace of the sky
Where great golden wonders never die.

The poem shows the Master with his work done, singing to free his heart in Heaven.

This poem is intended to be half said, half sung, very softly, to the well-known tune:—

"Last night I lay a-sleeping,
There came a dream so fair,
I stood in Old Jerusalem
Beside the temple there,—" etc.

Yet this tune is not to be fitted on, arbitrarily. It is here given to suggest the manner of handling rather than determine it.

I heard Immanuel singing *To be sung.*
Within his own good lands,
I saw him bend above his harp.
I watched his wandering hands
Lost amid the harp-strings;
Sweet, sweet I heard him play.
His wounds were altogether healed.
Old things had passed away.

All things were new, but music.
The blood of David ran
Within the Son of David,
Our God, the Son of Man.
He was ruddy like a shepherd.
His bold young face, how fair.
Apollo of the silver bow
Had not such flowing hair.

I saw Immanuel singing *To be read*
On a tree-girdled hill. *very softly,*
The glad remembering branches *but in spirited*
Dimly echoed still *response.*
The grand new song proclaiming

The Lamb that had been slain.
New-built, the Holy City
Gleamed in the murmuring plain.

The crowning hours were over.
The pageants all were past.
Within the many mansions
The hosts, grown still at last,
In homes of holy mystery
Slept long by crooning springs
Or waked to peaceful glory,
A universe of Kings.

To be sung.   He left his people happy.
He wandered free to sigh
Alone in lowly friendship
With the green grass and the sky.
He murmured ancient music
His red heart burned to sing
Because his perfect conquest
Had grown a weary thing.

No chant of gilded triumph—
His lonely song was made
Of Art's deliberate freedom;
Of minor chords arrayed
In soft and shadowy colors
That once were radiant flowers:—
The Rose of Sharon, bleeding
In Olive-shadowed bowers:—

And all the other roses
In the songs of East and West
Of love and war and worshipping,
And every shield and crest
Of thistle or of lotus
Or sacred lily wrought
In creeds and psalms and palaces
And temples of white thought:—

All these he sang, half-smiling
And weeping as he smiled,
Laughing, talking to his harp
As to a new-born child:—
As though the arts forgotten
But bloomed to prophesy
These careless, fearless harp-strings,
New-crying in the sky.

*To be read
very softly,
yet in spirited
response.*

"When this his hour of sorrow
For flowers and Arts of men
Has passed in ghostly music,"
I asked my wild heart then—
What will he sing tomorrow,
What wonder, all his own
Alone, set free, rejoicing
With a green hill for his throne?
What will he sing tomorrow
What wonder all his own
Alone, set free, rejoicing,
With a green hill for his throne?

To be sung.

❧ THE PRAIRIE BATTLEMENTS

(To Edgar Lee Masters, with great respect)

Here upon the prairie
Is our ancestral hall.
Agate is the dome,
Cornelian the wall.
Ghouls are in the cellar,
But fays upon the stairs.
And here lived old King Silver Dreams,
Always at his prayers.

Here lived gray Queen Silver Dreams,
Always singing psalms,
And haughty Grandma Silver Dreams,
Throned with folded palms.
Here played cousin Alice.
Her soul was best of all.
And every fairy loved her,
In our ancestral hall.

Alice has a prairie grave.
The King and Queen lie low,
And aged Grandma Silver Dreams,
Four tombstones in a row.
But still in snow and sunshine
Stands our ancestral hall.

Agate is the dome,
Cornelian the wall.
And legends walk about,
And proverbs, with proud airs.
Ghouls are in the cellar,
But fays upon the stairs.

FOREIGN MISSIONS
IN BATTLE ARRAY

An endless line of splendor,
These troops with heaven for home,
With creeds they go from Scotland,
With incense go from Rome.
These, in the name of Jesus,
Against the dark gods stand,
They gird the earth with valor,
They heed their King's command.

Onward the line advances,
Shaking the hills with power,
Slaying the hidden demons,
The lions that devour.
No bloodshed in the wrestling,—
But souls new-born arise—
The nations growing kinder,
The child-hearts growing wise.

What is the final ending?
The issue, can we know?
Will Christ outlive Mohammed?
Will Kali's altar go?
This is our faith tremendous,—
Our wild hope, who shall scorn,—
That in the name of Jesus
The world shall be reborn!

❧ AN ARGUMENT

I. The Voice of the Man Impatient with Visions and Utopias

We find your soft Utopias as white
As new-cut bread, and dull as life in cells,
O scribes who dare forget how wild we are,
How human breasts adore alarum bells.
You house us in a hive of prigs and saints
Communal, frugal, clean and chaste by law.
I'd rather brood in bloody Elsinore
Or be Lear's fool, straw-crowned amid the straw.
Promise us all our share in Agincourt
Say that our clerks shall venture scorns and death,
That future ant-hills will not be too good
For Henry Fifth, or Hotspur, or Macbeth.
Promise that through tomorrow's spirit-war
Man's deathless soul will hack and hew its way,
Each flaunting Cæsar climbing to his fate
Scorning the utmost steps of yesterday.
Never a shallow jester any more!
Let not Jack Falstaff spill the ale in vain.
Let Touchstone set the fashions for the wise
And Ariel wreak his fancies through the rain.

II. The Rhymer's Reply: Incense and Splendor

Incense and Splendor haunt me as I go.
Though my good works have been, alas, too few,
Though I do naught, High Heaven comes down to me,
And future ages pass in tall review.
I see the years to come as armies vast,
Stalking tremendous through the fields of time.

MAN is unborn. Tomorrow he is born,
Flame-like to hover o'er the moil and grime,
Striving, aspiring till the shame is gone,
Sowing a million flowers where now we mourn—
Laying new, precious pavements with a song,
Founding new shrines the good streets to adorn.
I have seen lovers by those new-built walls
Clothed like the dawn in orange, gold and red.
Eyes flashing forth the glory-light of love
Under the wreath that crowned each royal head.
Life was made greater by their sweetheart prayers.
Passion was turned to civic strength that day—
Piling the marbles, making fairer domes
With zeal that else had burned bright youth away.
I have seen priestesses of life go by,
Gliding the samite through the incense-sea—
Innocent children marching with them there,
Singing in flowered robes, "THE EARTH IS FREE":
While on the fair, deep-carved unfinished towers
Sentinels watched in armor, night and day—
Guarding the brazier-fires of hope and dream—
Wild was their peace, and dawn-bright their array!

❧ THE NORTH STAR WHISPERS
TO THE BLACKSMITH'S SON

The North Star whispers: "You are one
Of those whose course no chance can change.
You blunder, but are not undone,
Your spirit-task is fixed and strange.

"When here you walk, a bloodless shade,
A singer all men else forget.
Your chants of hammer, forge and spade
Will move the prairie-village yet.

"That young, stiff-necked, reviling town
Beholds your fancies on her walls,
And paints them out or tears them down,
Or bars them from her feasting-halls.

"Yet shall the fragments still remain;
Yet shall remain some watch-tower strong
That ivy-vines will not disdain,
Haunted and trembling with your song.

Section Three

RUNES OF THE
ROAD

I want to go wandering. Who shall declare
I will regret if I dare?

    To the rich days of age—
       To some mid-afternoon—
    A wide fenceless prairie,
       A lonely old tune,
    Ant-hills and sunflowers,
       And sunset too soon.

    Behind the brown mountain
       The sun will go down;
    I shall climb, I shall climb,
       To the sumptuous crown;
    To the rocks of the summit,
       And find some strange things:—
    Some echo of echoes
       When the thunder-wind sings;
    Old Spanish necklaces,
       Indian rings,
    Or a feeble old eagle
       With great, dragging wings.
    He may leave me and soar;
       But if he shall die,
    I shall bury him deep
       While the thunder-winds cry.

And there, as the last of my earth-nights go:
What is the thing I shall know?
With a feather cast off from his wings
I shall write, be it revel or psalm,
Or whisper of redwood, or cypress, or palm,—
The treasure of dream that he brings.

The soul of the eagle will call,
Whether he lives or he dies:—
The cliff and the prairie call,
The sagebrush and starlight sing,
And the songs of my far-away Sangamon call
From the plume of the bird of the Rockies,
And midnight's omnipotent wing—
The last of my earth-nights will ring
With cries from a far haunted river,
And all of my wandering,
      Wandering,
      Wandering,
      Wandering. . . .

❦ PROLOGUE TO "RHYMES

TO BE TRADED FOR BREAD"

(A Private Publication Out of Print)

Even the shrewd and bitter,
Gnarled by the old world's greed,
Cherished the stranger softly
Seeing his utter need.
Shelter and patient hearing,
These were their gifts to him,
To the minstrel chanting, begging,
As the sunset-fire grew dim.
The rich said "You are welcome."
Yea, even the rich were good.
How strange that in their feasting
His songs were understood!
The doors of the poor were open,
The poor who had wandered too,
Who slept with never a roof-tree
Under the wind and dew.
The minds of the poor were open,
There dark mistrust was dead:
They loved his wizard stories,
They bought his rhymes with bread.

Those were his days of glory,
Of faith in his fellow-men.
Therefore, to-day the singer
Turns beggar once again.

Sometimes we remember kisses,
Remember the dear heart-leap when they came:
Not always, but sometimes we remember
The kindness, the dumbness, the good flame
Of laughter and farewell.

                      Beside the road
Afar from those who said "Good-by" I write,
Far from my city task, my lawful load.

Sun in my face, wind beside my shoulder,
Streaming clouds, banners of new-born night
Enchant me now. The splendors growing bolder
Make bold my soul for some new wise delight.

I write the day's event, and quench my drouth,
Pausing beside the spring with happy mind.
And now I feel those kisses on my mouth,
Hers most of all, one little friend most kind.

❧ ON THE ROAD TO NOWHERE

On the road to nowhere
What wild oats did you sow
When you left your father's house
With your cheeks aglow?
Eyes so strained and eager
To see what you might see?
Were you thief or were you fool
Or most nobly free?

Were the tramp-days knightly,
True sowing of wild seed?
Did you dare to make the songs
Vanquished workmen need?
Did you waste much money
To deck a leper's feast?
Love the truth, defy the crowd
Scandalize the priest?
On the road to nowhere
What wild oats did you sow?
Stupids find the nowhere-road
Dusty, grim and slow.

Ere their sowing's ended
They turn them on their track,
Look at the caitiff craven wights
Repentant, hurrying back!
Grown ashamed of nowhere,
Of rags endured for years,
Lust for velvet in their hearts,
Pierced with Mammon's spears,
All but a few fanatics
Give up their darling goal,
Seek to be as others are,

Stultify the soul.
Reapings now confront them,
Glut them, or destroy.
Curious seeds, grain or weeds
Sown with awful joy.
Hurried is their harvest,
They make soft peace with men.
Pilgrims pass. They care not,
Will not tramp again.

O nowhere, golden nowhere!
Sages and fools go on
To your chaotic ocean,
To your tremendous dawn.
Far in your fair dream-haven,
Is nothing or is all . . .
They press on, singing, sowing
Wild deeds without recall!

Kiss me and comfort my heart
    Maiden honest and fine.
I am the pilgrim boy
    Lame, but hunting the shrine;

Fleeing away from the sweets,
    Seeking the dust and rain,
Sworn to the staff and road,
    Scorning pleasure and pain;

Nevertheless my mouth
    Would rest like a bird an hour
And find in your curls a nest
    And find in your breast a bower:

Nevertheless my eyes
    Would lose themselves in your own,
Rivers that seek the sea,
    Angels before the throne:

Kiss me and comfort my heart,
    For love can never be mine;
Passion, hunger and pain,
    These are the only wine

Of the pilgrim bound to the road.
    He would rob no man of his own.
Your heart is another's, I know,
    Your honor is his alone.

The feast of a long-drawn love,
    The feasts of a wedded life,

The harvests of patient years,
    And hearthstone and children and wife:

These are your lords, I know.
    These can never be mine—
This is the price I pay
    For the foolish search for the shrine:

This is the price I pay
    For the joy of my midnight prayers,
Kneeling beneath the moon
    With hills for my altar stairs;

This is the price I pay
    For the throb of the mystic wings.
When the dove of God comes down
    And beats round my heart and sings;

This is the price I pay
    For the light I shall some day see
At the ends of the infinite earth
    When truth shall come to me.

And what if my body die
    Before I meet the truth?
The road is dear, more dear
    Than love or life or youth.

The road, it is the road,
    Mystical, endless, kind,
Mother of visions vast,
    Mother of soul and mind;

Mother of all of me
    But the blood that cries for a mate—
That cries for a farewell kiss
    From the child of God at the gate.

🐟 THE WOULD-BE MERMAN

Mobs are like the Gulf Stream,
Like the vast Atlantic.
In your fragile boats you ride,
Conceited folk at ease.
Far beneath are dancers,
Mermen wild and frantic,
Circling round the giant glowing
Sea-anemones.

"Crude, ill-smelling voters,—
Herds," to you in seeming.
But to me their draggled clothes
Are scales of gold and red.
Ah, the pink sea-horses,
Green sea-dragons gleaming,
And knights that chase the dragons
And spear them till they're dead!

Wisdom waits the diver
In the social ocean—
Rainbow shells of wonder,
Piled into a throne.
I would go exploring
Through the wide commotion,
Building under some deep cliff
A pearl-throne all my own.

Yesterday I dived there,
Grinned at all the roaring,
Clinging to the corals for a flash,
Defying death.
Mermen came rejoicing,

In procession pouring,
Yet I lost my feeble grip
'And came above for breath.

I would be a merman.
Not in desperation
A momentary diver
Blue for lack of air.
But with gills deep-breathing
Swim amid the nation—
Finny feet and hands forsooth,
Sea-laurels in my hair.

❦ HONOR AMONG SCAMPS

We are the smirched. Queen Honor is the spotless.
We slept thro' wars where Honor could not sleep.
We were faint-hearted. Honor was full-valiant.
We kept a silence Honor could not keep.

Yet this late day we make a song to praise her.
We, codeless, will yet vindicate her code.
She who was mighty, walks with us, the beggars.
The merchants drive her out upon the road.

She makes a throne of sod beside our campfire.
We give the maiden-queen our rags and tears.
A battered, rascal guard have rallied round her,
To keep her safe until the better years.

(What Mister Moon Said to Me)

Come, eat the bread of idleness,
Come, sit beside the spring:
Some of the flowers will keep awake,
Some of the birds will sing.

Come, eat the bread no man has sought
For half a hundred years:
Men hurry so they have no griefs,
Nor even idle tears:

They hurry so they have no loves:
They cannot curse nor laugh—
Their hearts die in their youth with neither
Grave nor epitaph.

My bread would make them careless,
And never quite on time—
Their eyelids would be heavy,
Their fancies full of rhyme:

Each soul a mystic rose-tree,
Or a curious incense tree:

. . .

Come, eat the bread of idleness,
Said Mister Moon to me.

❦ THE BRONCHO THAT WOULD NOT BE BROKEN

A little colt—broncho, loaned to the farm
To be broken in time without fury or harm,
Yet black crows flew past you, shouting alarm,
Calling "Beware," with lugubrious singing . . .
The butterflies there in the bush were romancing,
The smell of the grass caught your soul in a trance,
So why be a-fearing the spurs and the traces,
O broncho that would not be broken of dancing?

You were born with the pride of the lords great and olden
Who danced, through the ages, in corridors golden.
In all the wide farm-place the person most human.
You spoke out so plainly with squealing and capering,
With whinnying, snorting contorting and prancing,
As you dodged your pursuers, looking askance,
With Greek-footed figures, and Parthenon paces,
O broncho that would not be broken of dancing.

The grasshoppers cheered. "Keep whirling," they said.
The insolent sparrows called from the shed
"If men will not laugh, make them wish they were dead."
But arch were your thoughts, all malice displacing,
Though the horse-killers came, with snake-whips advanc-
    ing
You bantered and cantered away your last chance.
And they scourged you, with Hell in their speech and their
    faces,
O broncho that would not be broken of dancing.

"Nobody cares for you," rattled the crows,
As you dragged the whole reaper, next day, down the rows.

The three mules held back, yet you danced on your toes.
You pulled like a racer, and kept the mules chasing,
You tangled the harness with bright eyes side-glancing,
While the drunk driver bled you—a pole for a lance—
And the giant mules bit at you—keeping their places.
O broncho that would not be broken of dancing.

In that last afternoon your boyish heart broke.
The hot wind came down like a sledge-hammer stroke.
The blood-sucking flies to a rare feast awoke.
And they searched out your wounds, your death-warrent
     tracing.
And the merciful men, their religion enhancing,
Stopped the red reaper, to give you a chance.
Then you died on the prairie, and scorned all disgraces,
O broncho that would not be broken of dancing.

Souvenir of Great Bend, Kansas.

I went down into the desert
To meet Elijah—
Arisen from the dead.
I thought to find him in an echoing cave;
For so my dream had said.

I went down into the desert
To meet John the Baptist.
I walked with feet that bled,
Seeking that prophet lean and brown and bold.
I spied foul fiends instead.

I went down into the desert
To meet my God.
By him be comforted.
I went down into the desert
To meet my God.
And I met the devil in red.

I went down into the desert
To meet my God.
O Lord my God, awaken from the dead!
I see you there, your thorn-crown on the ground,
I see you there, half-buried in the sand.
I see you there, your white bones glistening bare
The carrion-birds a-wheeling round your head.

The Moon's a devil-jester
Who makes himself too free.
The rascal is not always
Where he appears to be:—
Sometimes he is in my heart—
Sometimes in the sea.
Then tides are in my heart,
And tides are in the sea.
O traveler! abiding not
Where he pretends to be!

Section Four

POLITICS

OUR MOTHER POCAHONTAS

(NOTE:—*Pocahontas is buried at Gravesend, England*)

"Pocahontas' body, lovely as a poplar, sweet as a red haw in November or a pawpaw in May—did she wonder? does she remember—in the dust—in the cool tombs?"—Carl Sandburg

1

Powhatan was conqueror,
Powhatan was emperor.
He was akin to wolf and bee,
Brother of the hickory tree.
Son of the red lightning stroke
And the lightning-shivered oak.
His panther-grace bloomed in the maid
Who laughed among the winds and played
In excellence of savage pride,
Wooing the forest, open-eyed,
In the springtime,
In Virginia,
Our Mother, Pocahontas.
Her skin was rosy copper-red.
And high she held her beauteous head.
Her step was like a rustling leaf:
Her heart a nest, untouched of grief.
She dreamed of sons like Powhatan,
And through her blood the lightning ran.
Love-cries with the birds she sung,
Birdlike
In the grape-vine swung.
The Forest, arching low and wide
Gloried in its Indian bride.

Rolfe, that dim adventurer,
Had not come a courtier.
John Rolfe is not our ancestor.
We rise from out the soul of her
Held in native wonderland,
While the sun's rays kissed her hand,
In the springtime,
In Virginia,
Our Mother, Pocahontas.

II

She heard the forest talking,
And from her grave came walking,
Across the sea came walking,
And traced the paths of Daniel Boone,
Then westward chased the painted moon.
She passed with wild young feet
On to Kansas wheat,
On to the miners' west,
The echoing cañons' guest,
Then the Pacific sand,
Waking,
Thrilling,
The midnight land. . . .

On Adams Street and Jefferson—
Flames coming up from the ground!
On Jackson Street and Washington—
Flames coming up from the ground!
And why, until the dawning sun
Are flames coming up from the ground?
Because, through drowsy Springfield sped
This redskin queen, with feathered head,
With winds and stars, that pay her court
And leaping beasts, that make her sport;
Because, gray Europe's rags august

She tramples in the dust;
Because we are her fields of corn;
Because our fires are all reborn
From her bosom's deathless embers,
Flaming
As she remembers
The springtime
And Virginia,
Our Mother, Pocahontas.

III

We here renounce our Saxon blood.
Tomorrow's hopes, an April flood
Come roaring in. The newest race
Is born of her resilient grace.
We here renounce our Teuton pride:
Our Norse and Slavic boasts have died:
Italian dreams are swept away,
And Celtic feuds are lost today. . . .
She sings of lilacs, maples, wheat,
Her own soil sings beneath her feet,
Of springtime
And Virginia,
Our Mother, Pocahontas.

BRYAN, BRYAN, BRYAN, BRYAN

There are plenty of sweeping, swinging, stinging, gorgeous
things to shout about,
And knock your old blue devils out.

I brag and chant of Bryan, Bryan, Bryan,
Candidate for president who sketched a silver Zion,
The one American Poet who could sing outdoors,
He brought in tides of wonder, of unprecedented splendor,
Wild roses from the plains, that made hearts tender,
All the funny circus silks
Of politics unfurled,
Bartlett pears of romance that were honey at the cores,
And torchlights down the street, to the end of the world.

There were truths eternal in the gab and tittle-tattle.
There were real heads broken in the fustian and the rattle.
There were real lines drawn:
Not the silver and the gold,
But Nebraska's cry went eastward against the dour and old,
The mean and cold.

It was eighteen ninety-six, and I was just sixteen
And Altgeld ruled in Springfield, Illinois,
When there came from the sunset Nebraska's shout of joy:
In a coat like a deacon, in a black Stetson hat
He scourged the elephant plutocrats
With barbed wire from the Platte.
The scales dropped from their mighty eyes.
They saw that summer's noon
A tribe of wonders coming
To a marching tune.

Oh, the longhorns from Texas,
The jay hawks from Kansas,

The plop-eyed bungaroo and giant giassicus,
The varmint, chipmunk, bugaboo,
The horned-toad, prairie-dog and ballyhoo,
From all the newborn states arow,
Bidding the eagles of the west fly on,
Bidding the eagles of the west fly on.
The fawn, prodactyl and thing-a-ma-jig,
The rakaboor, the hellangone,
The whangdoodle, batfowl and pig,
The coyote, wild-cat and grizzly in a glow,
In a miracle of health and speed, the whole breed abreast,
They leaped the Mississippi, blue border of the West,
From the Gulf to Canada, two thousand miles long:—
Against the towns of Tubal Cain,
Ah,—sharp was their song.
Against the ways of Tubal Cain, too cunning for the young,
The longhorn calf, the buffalo and wampus gave tongue.

These creatures were defending things Mark Hanna never
     dreamed:
The moods of airy childhood that in desert dews gleamed,
The gossamers and whimsies,
The monkeyshines and didoes
Rank and strange
Of the canyons and the range,
The ultimate fantastics
Of the far western slope,
And of prairie schooner children
Born beneath the stars,
Beneath falling snows,
Of the babies born at midnight
In the sod huts of lost hope,
With no physician there,
Except a Kansas prayer,
With the Indian raid a-howling through the air.

And all these in their helpless days
By the dour East oppressed,

119

Mean paternalism
Making their mistakes for them,
Crucifying half the West,
Till the whole Atlantic coast
Seemed a giant spiders' nest.

And these children and their sons
At last rode through the cactus,
A cliff of mighty cowboys
On the lope,
With gun and rope.
And all the way to frightened Maine the old East heard
    them call,
And saw our Bryan by a mile lead the wall
Of men and whirling flowers and beasts,
The bard and the prophet of them all.
Prairie avenger, mountain lion,
Bryan, Bryan, Bryan, Bryan,
Gigantic troubadour, speaking like a siege gun,
Smashing Plymouth Rock with his boulders from the West,
And just a hundred miles behind, tornadoes piled across the
    sky,
Blotting out sun and moon,
A sign on high.

Headlong, dazed and blinking in the weird green light,
The scalawags made moan,
Afraid to fight.

II

When Bryan came to Springfield, and Altgeld gave him
    greeting,
Rochester was deserted, Divernon was deserted,
Mechanicsburg, Riverton, Chickenbristle, Cotton Hill,
Empty: for all Sangamon drove to the meeting—

In silver-decked racing cart,
Buggy, buckboard, carryall,
Carriage, phaeton, whatever would haul,
And silver-decked farm-wagons gritted, banged and rolled,
With the new tale of Bryan by the iron tires told.

The State House loomed afar,
A speck, a hive, a football,
A captive balloon!
And the town was all one spreading wing of bunting,
    plumes, and sunshine,
Every rag and flag, and Bryan picture sold,
When the rigs in many a dusty line
Jammed our streets at noon,
And joined the wild parade against the power of gold.

We roamed, we boys from High School,
With mankind,
While Springfield gleamed,
Silk-lined.
Oh, Tom Dines, and Art Fitzgerald,
And the gangs that they could get!
I can hear them yelling yet.
Helping the incantation,
Defying aristocracy,
With every bridle gone,
Ridding the world of the low down mean,
Bidding the eagles of the West fly on,
Bidding the eagles of the West fly on,
We were bully, wild and woolly,
Never yet curried below the knees.
We saw flowers in the air,
Fair as the Pleiades, bright as Orion,
—Hopes of all mankind,
Made rare, resistless, thrice refined.
Oh, we bucks from every Springfield ward!
Colts of democracy—

Yet time-winds out of Chaos from the star-fields of the
     Lord.

The long parade rolled on. I stood by my best girl.
She was a cool young citizen, with wise and laughing eyes.
With my necktie by my ear, I was stepping on my dear,
But she kept like a pattern, without a shaken curl.

She wore in her hair a brave prairie rose.
Her gold chums cut her, for that was not the pose.
No Gibson Girl would wear it in that fresh way.
But we were fairy Democrats, and this was our day.

The earth rocked like the ocean, the sidewalk was a deck.
The houses for the moment were lost in the wide wreck.
And the bands played strange and stranger music as they
     trailed along.
Against the ways of Tubal Cain,
Ah, sharp was their song!
The demons in the bricks, the demons in the grass,
The demons in the bank-vaults peered out to see us pass,
And the angels in the trees, the angels in the grass,
The angels in the flags, peered out to see us pass.
And the sidewalk was our chariot, and the flowers bloomed
     higher,
And the street turned to silver and the grass turned to fire,
And then it was but grass, and the town was there again,
A place for women and men.

III

Then we stood where we could see
Every band,
And the speaker's stand.
And Bryan took the platform.
And he was introduced.

And he lifted his hand
And cast a new spell.
Progressive silence fell
In Springfield,
In Illinois,
Around the world.
Then we heard these glacial boulders across the prairie
    rolled:
"The people have a right to make their own mistakes. . . .
You shall not crucify mankind
Upon a cross of gold."

And everybody heard him—
In the streets and State House yard.
And everybody heard him
In Springfield,
In Illinois,
Around and around and around the world,
That danced upon its axis
And like a darling broncho whirled.

IV

July, August, suspense.
Wall Street lost to sense.
August, September, October,
More suspense,
And the whole East down like a wind-smashed fence.

Then Hanna to the rescue,
Hanna of Ohio,
Rallying the roller-tops,
Rallying the bucket-shops.
Threatening drouth and death,
Promising manna,
Rallying the trusts against the bawling flannelmouth;
Invading misers' cellars,
Tin-cans, socks,

Melting down the rocks,
Pouring out the long green to a million workers,
Spondulix by the mountain-load, to stop each new tornado,
And beat the cheapskate, blatherskite,
Populistic, anarchistic,
Deacon—desperado.

V

Election night at midnight:
Boy Bryan's defeat.
Defeat of western silver.
Defeat of the wheat.
Victory of letterfiles
And plutocrats in miles
With dollar signs upon their coats,
Diamond watchchains on their vests
And spats on their feet.
Victory of custodians,
Plymouth Rock,
And all that inbred landlord stock.
Victory of the neat.
Defeat of the aspen groves of Colorado valleys,
The blue bells of the Rockies,
And blue bonnets of old Texas,
By the Pittsburg alleys.
Defeat of alfalfa and the Mariposa lily.
Defeat of the Pacific and the long Mississippi.
Defeat of the young by the old and silly.
Defeat of tornadoes by the poison vats supreme.
Defeat of my boyhood, defeat of my dream.

VI

Where is McKinley, that respectable McKinley,
The man without an angle or a tangle,

Who soothed down the city man and soothed down the
  farmer,
The German, the Irish, the Southerner, the Northerner,
Who climbed every greasy pole, and slipped through every
  crack;
Who soothed down the gambling hall, the bar-room, the
  church,
The devil vote, the angel vote, the neutral vote,
The desperately wicked, and their victims on the rack,
The gold vote, the silver vote, the brass vote, the lead vote,
Every vote? . . .

Where is McKinley, Mark Hanna's McKinley,
His slave, his echo, his suit of clothes?
Gone to join the shadows, with the pomps of that time,
And the flame of that summer's prairie rose.

Where is Cleveland whom the Democratic platform
Read from the party in a glorious hour,
Gone to join the shadows with pitchfork Tillman,
And sledge-hammer Altgeld who wrecked his power.

Where is Hanna, bulldog Hanna.
Low-browed Hanna, who said: "Stand pat"?
Gone to his place with old Pierpont Morgan.
Gone somewhere . . . with lean rat Platt.

Where is Roosevelt, the young dude cowboy,
Who hated Bryan, then aped his way?
Gone to join the shadows with mighty Cromwell
And tall King Saul, till the Judgment day.

Where is Altgeld, brave as the truth,
Whose name the few still say with tears?
Gone to join the ironies with Old John Brown,
Whose fame rings loud for a thousand years.

Where is that boy, that Heaven-born Bryan,
That Homer Bryan, who sang from the West?
Gone to join the shadows with Altgeld the Eagle,
Where the kings and the slaves and the troubadours rest.

Written at the Guanella Ranch, Empire, Colorado, August,
  1919.

⚑ THE STATUE OF OLD
ANDREW JACKSON

(Written while America was in the midst of the war with Germany, August, 1918)

When the statue of Andrew Jackson before the White House in Washington is removed, America is doomed. The nobler days of America's innocence, in which it was set up, always have a special tang for those who are tasty. But this is not all. It is only the America that has the courage of her complete past that can hold up her head in the world of the artists, priests and sages. It is for us to put the iron dog and deer back upon the lawn, the John Rogers group back into the parlor, and get new inspiration from these and from Andrew Jackson ramping in bronze replica in New Orleans, Nashville and Washington, and add to them a sense of humor, till it becomes a sense of beauty that will resist the merely dulcet and affettuoso.

Please read Lorado Taft's *History of American Sculpture*, pages 123–127, with these matters in mind. I quote a few bits:

". . . The maker of the first equestrian statue in the history of American sculpture: Clark Mills. . . . Never having seen General Jackson or an equestrian statue, he felt himself incompetent . . . the incident, however, made an impression on his mind, and he reflected sufficiently to produce a design which was the very one subsequently executed. . . . Congress appropriated the old cannon captured by General Jackson. . . . Having no notion, nor even suspicion of a dignified sculptural treatment of a theme, the clever carpenter felt, nevertheless, the need of a feature. . . . He built a colossal horse, adroitly balanced on the hind legs, and America gazed with bated breath. Nobody knows or cares whether the rider looks like Jackson or not.

"The extraordinary pose of the horse absorbs all attention, all admiration. There may be some subconscious feeling of respect for a rider who holds on so well. . . ."

Andrew Jackson was eight feet tall.
His arm was a hickory limb and a maul.
His sword was so long he dragged it on the ground.
Every friend was an equal. Every foe was a hound.

Andrew Jackson was a Democrat,
Defying kings in his old cocked hat.
His vast steed rocked like a hobby-horse.
But he sat straight up. He held his course.

He licked the British at Noo Orleans;
Beat them out of their elegant jeans.
He piled the cotton-bales twenty feet high,
And he snorted "freedom," and it flashed from his eye.

And the American Eagle swooped through the air,
And cheered when he heard the Jackson swear:—
"By the Eternal, let them come.
Sound Yankee Doodle. Let the bullets hum."

And his wild men, straight from the woods, fought on
Till the British fops were dead and gone.

And now old Andrew Jackson fights
To set the sad big world to rights.
He joins the British and the French.
He cheers up the Italian trench.
He's making Democrats of these,
And freedom's sons of Japanese.
His hobby horse will gallop on
Till all the infernal Huns are gone.

Yes,
Yes,
Yes!
By the Eternal!
Old Andrew Jackson!

ABRAHAM LINCOLN WALKS
AT MIDNIGHT

(In Springfield, Illinois)

It is portentous, and a thing of state
That here at midnight, in our little town
A mourning figure walks, and will not rest,
Near the old court-house pacing up and down,

Or by his homestead, or in shadowed yards
He lingers where his children used to play,
Or through the market, on the well-worn stones
He stalks until the dawn-stars burn away.

A bronzed, lank man! His suit of ancient black,
A famous high top-hat and plain worn shawl
Make him the quaint great figure that men love,
The prairie-lawyer, master of us all.

He cannot sleep upon his hillside now.
He is among us:—as in times before!
And we who toss and lie awake for long
Breathe deep, and start, to see him pass the door.

His head is bowed. He thinks on men and kings.
Yea, when the sick world cries, how can he sleep?
Too many peasants fight, they know not why,
Too many homesteads in black terror weep.

The sins of all the war-lords burn his heart.
He see the dreadnaughts scouring every main.
He carries on his shawl-wrapped shoulders now
The bitterness, the folly and the pain.

He cannot rest until a spirit-dawn
Shall come;—the shining hope of Europe free:
The league of sober folk, the Workers' Earth,
Bringing long peace to Cornland, Alp and Sea.

It breaks his heart that kings must murder still,
That all his hours of travail here for men
Seem yet in vain. And who will bring white peace
That he may sleep upon his hill again?

✒ *THE EAGLE THAT IS FORGOTTEN*

(*John P. Altgeld. Born December 30, 1847; died March 12, 1902*)

Sleep softly . . . eagle forgotten . . . under the stone.
Time has its way with you there, and the clay has its own.

"We have buried him now," thought your foes, and in
   secret rejoiced.
They made a brave show of their mourning, their hatred
   unvoiced.

They had snarled at you, barked at you, foamed at you day
   after day.
Now you were ended. They praised you, . . . and laid you
   away.

The others that mourned you in silence and terror and
   truth,
The widow bereft of her crust, and the boy without youth,
The mocked and the scorned and the wounded, the lame
   and the poor
That should have remembered forever, . . . remember no
   more.

Where are those lovers of yours, on what name do they call
The lost, that in armies wept over your funeral pall?
They call on the names of a hundred high-valiant ones,
A hundred white eagles have risen the sons of your sons,
The zeal in their wings is a zeal that your dreaming began
The valor that wore out your soul in the service of man.

Sleep softly, . . . eagle forgotten, . . . under the stone,
Time has its way with you there and the clay has its own.

Sleep on, O brave-hearted, O wise man, that kindled the
flame—
To live in mankind is far more than to live in a name,
To live in mankind, far, far more . . . than to live in a
name.

IN WHICH ROOSEVELT IS COMPARED TO SAUL

(Written and published in 1913, and republished five years later, in the Boston Transcript, *on the death of Roosevelt)*

Where is David? . . . Oh God's people
Saul has passed, the good and great.
Mourn for Saul, the first anointed,
Head and shoulders o'er the state.

He was found among the prophets:
Judge and monarch, merged in one.
But the wars of Saul are ended,
And the works of Saul are done.

Where is David, ruddy shepherd,
God's boy-king for Israel?
Mystic, ardent, dowered with beauty.
Singing where still waters dwell?

Prophet, find that destined minstrel
Wandering on the range today,
Driving sheep, and crooning softly
Psalms that cannot pass away.

"David waits," the prophet answers,
"In a black, notorious den,
In a cave upon the border,
With four hundred outlaw men.

"He is fair and loved of women,
Mighty-hearted, born to sing:
Thieving, weeping, erring, praying,
Radiant royal rebel-king.

"He will come with harp and psaltry,
Quell his troop of convict swine,
Quell his mad-dog roaring rascals,
Witching them with tunes divine.

"They will ram the walls of Zion.
They will win us Salem hill,
All for David, shepherd David,
Singing like a mountain rill."

HAIL TO THE SONS
OF ROOSEVELT

"Out of the eater came forth meat, and out of the strong came forth sweetness."—Samson's riddle

There is no name for brother
Like the name of Jonathan
The son of Saul.
And so we greet you all:
The sons of Roosevelt—
The sons of Saul.

Four brother Jonathans went out to battle.
Let every Yankee poet sing their praise
Through all the days—
What David sang of Saul
And Jonathan, beloved more than all.

God grant such sons, begot of our young men,
To make each generation glad again.
Let sons of Saul be springing up again:
Out of the eater, fire and power again.
From the lost lion, honey for all men.

I hear the sacred Rocky Mountains call,
I hear the Mississippi Jordan call:
"Stand up, America, and praise them all,
Living and dead, the fine young sons of Saul!"

◢ ROOSEVELT

(Written for the Illinois State Teachers' Association, printed as a broadside, and read, and distributed the same day: April 4, 1924)

When the stuffed prophets quarrel, when the sawdust
        comes out, I think of Roosevelt's genuine sins.
Once more my rash love for that cinnamon bear,
    Begins!

His sins were better than their sweetest goodness.
His blows were cleaner than their plainest kindness.
He saw more than they all, in his hours of black blindness.
The hour of his pitiful spiritual fall
He was more of an angel than all of this host,
When with Lucifer's pride his soul was burnt out,
When, still in the game, he gave up the ghost.

His yarns were nearer the sky than their truth.
His wildest tales, in his fish-story hour,
Nearer true than their truth.
When with art and with laughter he held supreme power,
He was white as the moon, and as honest as youth.

And now their sworn word is but barnyard mud.
And their highest pride is to hide in a hole.
They talk of "dollars" and "dollars" and "dollars"
And "dollars" and "dollars," and hate his clean soul.

(Oh money, money—that *never* can think,
Money, money, that *never* can rule,
Always an anarchist, always an idiot,
Always King Log—never King Stork,
Always rotting, reeking:—always a fool.)

Roosevelt was proud like a singer.
Roosevelt's pride was that of a scribe,
Or the pride of a father, the pride of a ruler,
The pride of the thoroughbred chief of a tribe,
The pride of Confucius, the pride of a student!
He hated a coward, he hated a fool,
He knew that money is always a fool.

When they tear each others' newspaper-hearts
I think of Theodore's genuine code.
He hated the paste-board, the smeary, the fake.
He hated the snake, the frog and the toad.

Oh a moose with sharp antlers!
Oh a panther of panthers—Oh a fox of foxes
Often caught in tight boxes!
Yet we know he would always bark out the truth.
He loved the curious political game:—
But we know he loved better:—truth, God, and *youth*.

A peacock of peacocks! An eagle of eagles!
Defeating, within himself, the quick fox.
A buffalo roaring—a world-lion roaring!
Defeating within himself the bright fox,—
Then ranging out through the wilderness trail,
Killing the jackal—felling the ox.

Megalomaniac, envious, glorious,
Envying only the splendors of worth.

Emulating the cleanest on earth,
(Those who were, therefore, the strongest on earth).
Emulating thoroughbreds—always.
Peacock! Lion! Cinnamon bear!
Skyscrapers—steeples and plains for abode!
He was mostly the world's fine cinnamon bear,
He was mostly our glittering cinnamon bear,
Sitting there in an old rocking chair,
In the White House yard, taking the air.

He told us Aesop's new fables, each day—
President seven big glorious years!
Seven years of wonder. Must they all fade away,
In the quarrels of the rat with the loud-voiced cootie
Told by the zinc-throated, varnished "loud-speaker,"
Told by wireless, while the world sits breathless,
Or by megaphone,
By line-o'-type, or by letter ripe:—
The quarrels of the angle-worm with the toad?

Who elected these pole-cats rulers of men?

Let us start a gay nation over again!
Let us start a circus as honest as Barnum's,
With three clean rings, and plenty to see,
Athletes, not snakes, on the trapeze tree.

Let us start our nation over again,
In the names of legitimate rulers of men,
In the names of the great, and the famous dead:—
Yes, the name of the glittering cinnamon bear,
Never so wicked or sore in the head,
But he fed the children honey and bread.
He taught them the names of the great and the dead,
From the Irish Sagas, to Carson and Boone.

He loved the villages, Deadwood, Medora,
Tuskeegee and Tuscarora,
Mexicali and Farmington,
Calexico and Bennington,
Arlington and Lexington,
Oyster Bay, Mount Vernon.

He loved the cities Denver, Manhattan,
And the wide great spaces
From the Amazon to Saskatoon—
He loved the heroes, Columbus, Whitman, Lincoln,
He loved the heroes! He loved George Washington!—
Who was honest as youth and white as the moon.

"Great-heart!" Roosevelt! Father of men!
He fed the children honey and bread.
He taught them the Ten Commandments and prayer,
Rocking there in his old rocking chair,
Or riding the storms of dream that he rode.

Join hands, poets, friends, companions!
Let us start a new world on the Roosevelt Code!

Let us start our nation over again
In the name of the honest, proud cinnamon bear,
Rocking there in his old rocking chair
Or riding the terrible storms that he rode!

The most-quoted phrase from the first edition of this book is on page 2—"*That this whole book is a weapon in a strenuous battle-field.*" So this section starts with two broadsides, carrying out that idea, one on Roosevelt, one on Sandburg. "Roosevelt" was written, printed and issued in one day, after reading of the behavior of two middle western governors, that morning. I read the poem that night in East St. Louis for the Illinois State Teachers' Association, three thousand strong. It was distributed by the Doubleday Page Book Shop, St. Louis. I read it in the loudest voice I could muster, holding the broadside up before the convention like a banner. It was an occasion of some humor, but of even more seriousness, and the New Republic telegraphed for a copy of the broadside at once, and re-issued it in abbreviated form. In this form it was quoted with apparent approval by the Philadelphia *North American,* and sent for by the Roosevelt Memorial Association to be fastened on their walls. And the same day it was politically attacked by the earnest Providence (Rhode Island) *Journal.*

⚑ LOVE AND LAW

True Love is founded in rocks of Remembrance
In stones of Forbearance and mortar of Pain.
The workman lays wearily granite on granite,
And bleeds for his castle 'mid sunshine and rain.

Love is not velvet, not all of it velvet,
Not all of it banners, not gold-leaf alone.
'Tis stern as the ages and old as Religion.
With Patience its watchword, and Law for its throne.

✄ THE LEADEN-EYED

Let not young souls be smothered out before
They do quaint deeds and fully flaunt their pride.
It is the world's one crime its babes grow dull,
Its poor are ox-like, limp and leaden-eyed.

Not that they starve, but starve so dreamlessly,
Not that they sow, but that they seldom reap,
Not that they serve, but have no gods to serve,
Not that they die but that they die like sheep.

FACTORY WINDOWS ARE
ALWAYS BROKEN

Factory windows are always broken.
Somebody's always throwing bricks,
Somebody's always heaving cinders,
Playing ugly Yahoo tricks.

Factory windows are always broken.
Other windows are let alone.
No one throws through the chapel-window
The bitter, snarling, derisive stone.

Factory windows are always broken.
Something or other is going wrong.
Something is rotten—I think, in Denmark.
End of the factory-window song.

WHY I VOTED THE
SOCIALIST TICKET

I am unjust, but I can strive for justice.
My life's unkind, but I can vote for kindness.
I, the unloving, say life should be lovely.
I, that am blind, cry out against my blindness.

Man is a curious brute—he pets his fancies—
Fighting mankind, to win sweet luxury.
So he will be, tho' law be clear as crystal,
Tho' all men plan to live in harmony.

Come let us vote against our human nature,
Crying to God in all the polling places
To heal our everlasting sinfulness
And make us sages with transfigured faces.

Think not that incense-smoke has had its day.
My friends, the incense-time has but begun.
Creed upon creed, cult upon cult shall bloom,
Shrine after shrine grow gray beneath the sun.

And mountain-boulders in our aged West
Shall guard the graves of hermits truth-endowed:
And there the scholar from the Chinese hills
Shall do deep honor, with his wise head bowed.

And on our old, old plains some muddy stream,
Dark as the Ganges, shall, like that strange tide—
(Whispering mystery to half the earth)—
Gather the praying millions to its side,

And flow past halls with statues in white stone
To saints unborn today, whose lives of grace
Shall make one shining, universal church
Where all Faiths kneel, as brothers, in one place.

A NET TO SNARE
THE MOONLIGHT

(What the Man of Faith Said)

The dew, the rain and moonlight
All prove our Father's mind.
The dew, the rain and moonlight
Descend to bless mankind.

Come, let us see that all men
Have land to catch the rain,
Have grass to snare the spheres of dew,
And fields spread for the grain.

Yea, we would give to each poor man
Ripe wheat and poppies red,—
A peaceful place at evening
With the stars just overhead:

A net to snare the moonlight,
A sod to spread to the sun,
A place of toil by daytime,
Of dreams when toil is done.

✠ THE SOUL OF A SPIDER

The thing that eats the rotting stars
  On the black sea-beach of shame
Is a giant spider's deathless soul,
  And Mammon is its name.

WHAT THE HYENA SAID

The moon is but a golden skull,
She mounts the heavens now,
And Moon-Worms, mighty Moon-Worms
Are wreathed around her brow.

The Moon-Worms are a doughty race:
They eat her gray and golden face.
Her eye-sockets dead, and molding head:
These caverns are their dwelling-place.

The Moon-Worms, serpents of the skies,
From the great hollows of her eyes
Behold all souls, and they are wise:
With tiny, keen and icy eyes,
Behold how each man sins and dies.

When Earth in gold-corruption lies
Long dead, the moon-worm butterflies
On cyclone wings will reach this place—
Yea, rear their brood on earth's dead face.

◤ PARVENU

Where does Cinderella sleep?
By Heaven's jungle-river,
A secret place her burning Prince
Decks, while his heart-strings quiver.

Homesick for our cinder world,
Her low-born shoulders shiver;
She longs for sleep in cinders curled—
We, for the jungle-river.

THE WEDDING OF THE ROSE
AND THE LOTUS

*(A poem distributed to both houses of Congress by Secretary
Franklin K. Lane on the opening day of the Panama-Pacific
Exposition)*

Flags of the Pacific
And the Atlantic meet,
Captain calls to captain,
Fleet makes cheer with fleet.
Above the drownèd ages
A wind of wooing blows:—
The red rose woos the lotus,
The lotus woos the rose . . .

The lotus conquered Egypt.
      The rose was loved in Rome.
Great India crowned the lotus:
(Britain the rose's home).
Old China crowned the lotus,
They crowned it in Japan.
But Christendom adored the rose
Ere Christendom began . . .

The lotus speaks of slumber:
The rose is as a dart.
      The lotus is Nirvana:
The rose is Mary's heart.
The rose is deathless, restless,
The splendor of our pain:
      The flush and fire of labor
That builds, not all in vain. . . .

The genius of the lotus
Shall heal earth's too-much fret.
The rose, in blinding glory,
Shall waken Asia yet.
Hail to their loves, ye peoples!
Behold, a world-wind blows,
That aids the ivory lotus
To wed the red, red rose!

SEW THE FLAGS TOGETHER

(Written for William Stanley Braithwaite's Victory Anthology issued at once, after Armistice Day, November, 1918)

Great wave of youth, ere you be spent,
Sweep over every monument
Of caste, smash every high imperial wall
That stands against the new World State,
And overwhelm each ravening hate,
And heal, and make blood-brothers of us all.
Nor let your clamor cease
Till ballots conquer guns.
Drum on for the world's peace
Till the Tory power is gone.
Envenomed lame old age
Is not our heritage,
But springtime's vast release, and flaming dawn.

Peasants, rise in splendor
And your accounting render
Ere the lords unnerve your hand!
Sew the flags together.
Do not tear them down.
Hurl the worlds together.
Dethrone the wallowing monster
And the clown.
Resolving:—
"Only that shall grow
In Balkan furrow, Chinese row,
That blooms, and is perpetually young."
That only be held fine and dear
That brings heart-wisdom year by year
And puts this thrilling word upon the tongue:
"The United States of Europe, Asia, and the World."

"Youth will be served," now let us cry.
Hurl the referendum.
Your fathers, five long years ago,
Resolved to strike, too late.
Now
Sun-crowned crowds
Innumerable,
Of boys and girls
Imperial,
With your patchwork flag of brotherhood
On high,
With every silk
In one flower-banner whirled—
Rise,
Citizens of one tremendous state,
The United States of Europe, Asia, and the World.

The dawn is rose-drest and impearled.
The guards of privilege are spent.
The blood-fed captains nod.
So Saxon, Slav, French, German,
Rise,
Yankee, Chinese, Japanese,
All the lands, all the seas,
With the blazing rainbow flag unfurled,
Rise, rise.
Take the sick dragons by surprise,
Highly establish,
In the name of God,
The United States of Europe, Asia, and the World.

⚑ *THE JINGO AND THE MINSTREL*

Glossary for the uninstructed and the hasty: Jimmu Tenno, ancestor of all the Japanese Emperors; Nikko, Japan's loveliest shrine; Iyeyasu, her greatest statesman; Bushido, her code of knighthood; The Forty-seven Ronins, her classic heroes; Nogi, her latest hero; Fuji, her most beautiful mountain. The Pendragon flag is King Arthur's Banner (see Tennyson).

An Argument for the Maintenance of Peace and Goodwill with the Japanese People

"Now do you know of Avalon
    That sailors call Japan?
She holds as rare a chivalry
    As ever bled for man.
King Arthur sleeps at Nikko hill
    Where Iyeyasu lies,
And there the broad Pendragon flag
    In deathless splendor flies."

The minstrel speaks.

*"Nay, minstrel, but the great ships come
    From out the sunset sea.
We cannot greet the souls they bring
    With welcome high and free.
How can the Nippon nondescripts,
    That weird and dreadful band,
Be aught but what we find them here:—
    The blasters of the land?"*

The jingo answers.

"First race, first men from anywhere
    To face you, eye to eye.
For *that* do you curse Avalon
    And raise a hue and cry?
These toilers cannot kiss your hand,

The minstrel replies.

153

Or fawn with hearts bowed down.
Be glad for them, and Avalon,
        And Arthur's ghostly crown.

"No doubt your guests, with sage debate,
        In grave things gentlemen,
Will let your trade and farms alone,
        And turn them back again.
But why should brawling braggarts rise
        With hasty words of shame,
To drive them back, like dogs and swine,
        Who in due honor came?"

The jingo answers.

*"We cannot give them honor, sir.
        We give them scorn for scorn.
And Rumor steals around the world,
        All white-skinned men to warn
Against this sleek silk-merchant here
        And viler coolie-man,
And wrath within the courts of war
        Brews on against Japan!"*

The minstrel replies.

"Must Avalon, with hope forlorn,
        Her back against the wall,
Have lived her brilliant life in vain
        While ruder tribes take all?
Must Arthur stand with Asian Celts,
        A ghost with spear and crown,
Behind the great Pendragon flag
        And be again cut down?

"Tho' Europe's self shall move against
        High Jimmu Tenno's throne,
The Forty-seven Ronin Men
        Will not be found alone.
For Percival and Bedivere
        And Nogi side by side
Will stand,—with mourning Merlin there,
        Tho' all go down in pride.

154

"But has the world the envious dream—
    Ah, such things cannot be,—
To tear their fairy-land like silk
    And toss it in the sea?
Must this day rob the future day,
    The ultimate world-man,
Of rare Bushido, code of codes,
    The fair heart of Japan?

"Go, be the guest of Avalon.
    Believe me it lies there
Behind the mighty gray sea-wall
    Where heathen bend in prayer:
Where peasants lift adoring eyes
    To Fuji's crown of snow.
King Arthur's knights will be your hosts,
    So cleanse your heart, and go.

"And you will find but gardens sweet
    Prepared beyond the seas,
And you will find but gentlefolk
    Beneath the cherry-trees.
So walk you worthy of your Christ
    The church bells do not sound,
And weave the bands of brotherhood
    On Jimmu Tenno's ground."

THE VOICE OF ST. FRANCIS OF ASSISI

I saw St. Francis by a stream
Washing his wounds that bled.
The aspens quivered overhead.
The silver doves flew round.
Weeping and sore dismayed
"Peace, peace," St. Francis prayed.

But the soft doves quickly fled.
Carrion crows flew round.
An earthquake rocked the ground.

"War, war," the west wind said.

A CURSE FOR KINGS

A curse upon each king who leads his state,
No matter what his plea, to this foul game,
And may it end his wicked dynasty,
And may he die in exile and black shame.

If there is vengeance in the Heaven of Heavens,
What punishment could Heaven devise for these
Who fill the rivers of the world with dead,
And turn their murderers loose on all the seas!

Put back the clock of time a thousand years,
And make our Europe, once the world's proud Queen,
A shrieking strumpet, furious fratricide,
Eater of entrails, wallowing obscene

In pits where millions foam and rave and bark,
Mad dogs and idiots, thrice drunk with strife;
While Science towers above;—a witch, red-winged:
Science we looked to for the light of life.

Curse me the men who make and sell iron ships,
Who walk the floor in thought, that they may find
Each powder prompt, each steel with fearful edge,
Each deadliest device against mankind.

Curse me the sleek lords with their plumes and spurs,
May Heaven give their land to peasant spades,
Give them the brand of Cain, for their pride's sake,
And felon's stripes for medals and for braids.

Curse me the fiddling, twiddling diplomats,
Haggling here, plotting and hatching there,
Who make the kind world but their game of cards,
Till millions die at turning of a hair.

157

What punishment will Heaven devise for these
Who win by others' sweat and hardihood,
Who make men into stinking vultures' meat,
Saying to evil still "Be thou my good"?

Ah, he who starts a million souls toward death
Should burn in utmost hell a million years!
—Mothers of men go on the destined wrack
To give them life, with anguish and with tears:—

Are all those childbed sorrows sneered away?
Yea, fools laugh at the humble christenings,
And cradle-joys are mocked of the fat lords:
These mothers' sons made dead men for the Kings!

All in the name of this or that grim flag,
No angel-flags in all the rag-array—
Banners the demons love, and all Hell sings
And plays wild harps. Those flags march forth today!

WHO KNOWS?

They say one king is mad. Perhaps. Who knows?
They say one king is doddering and gray.
They say one king is slack and sick of mind,
A puppet for hid strings that twitch and play.

Is Europe then to be their sprawling-place?
Their madhouse, till it turns the wide world's bane?
Their place of maudlin, slavering conference
Till every far-off farmstead goes insane?

✒ THE UNPARDONABLE SIN

This is the sin against the Holy Ghost:—
To speak of bloody power as right divine,
And call on God to guard each vile chief's house,
And for such chiefs, turn men to wolves and swine:—

To go forth killing in White Mercy's name,
Making the trenches stink with spattered brains,
Tearing the nerves and arteries apart,
Sowing with flesh the unreaped golden plains.

In any Church's name, to sack fair towns,
And turn each home into a screaming sty,
To make the little children fugitive,
And have their mothers for a quick death cry,—

This is the sin against the Holy Ghost:
This is the sin no purging can atone:—
To send forth rapine in the name of Christ:—
To set the face, and make the heart a stone.

✍ THE MERCIFUL HAND

(Written to Miss Alice L. F. Fitzgerald, Edith Cavell memorial nurse, going to the front)

Your fine white hand is Heaven's gift
To cure the wide world, stricken sore,
Bleeding at the breast and head,
Tearing at its wounds once more.

Your white hand is a prophecy,
A living hope that Christ shall come
And make the nations merciful,
Hating the bayonet and drum.

Each desperate burning brain you soothe,
Or ghastly broken frame you bind,
Brings one day nearer our bright goal,
The love-alliance of mankind.

WELLESLEY,
February, 1916.

☙ *WHERE IS THE REAL NON-RESISTANT?*

(Matthew V, 38–48)

Who can surrender to Christ, dividing his best with the
    stranger,
Giving to each what he asks, braving the uttermost danger
All for the enemy, MAN? Who can surrender till death
His words and his works, his house and his lands,
His eyes and his heart and his breath?

Who can surrender to Christ? Many have yearned toward
    it daily.
Yet they surrender to passion, wildly or grimly or gaily:
Yet they surrender to pride, counting her precious and
    queenly;
Yet they surrender to knowledge, preening their feathers
    serenely.

Who can surrender to Christ? Where is the man so tran-
    scendent,
So heated with love of his kind, so filled with the spirit
    resplendent
That all of the hours of his day his song is thrilling and
    tender,
And all of his thoughts to our white cause of peace
            Surrender, surrender, surrender?

SHANTUNG, OR THE EMPIRE
OF CHINA IS CRUMBLING DOWN

(Dedicated to William Rose Benét)

"Confucius appeared, according to Mencius, one of his most distinguished followers, at a crisis in the nation's history. 'The world,' he says, 'had fallen into decay, and right principles had disappeared. Perverse discourses and oppressive deeds were waxen rife. Ministers murdered their rulers, and sons their fathers. Confucius was frightened by what he saw,—and he undertook the work of reformation.'

"He was a native of the state of Lu, a part of the modern Shantung. . . . Lu had a great name among the other states of Chow . . . etc." Rev. James Legge, Professor of Chinese, University of Oxford.

I have found the poem Shantung an especial favorite with the audience when I have been called upon to recite for the staff of some public library.

I

Now let the generations pass—
Like sand through Heaven's blue hour-glass.

In old Shantung,
By the capital where poetry began,
Near the only printing presses known to man,
Young Confucius walks the shore
On a sorrowful day.
The town, all books, is tumbling down
Through the blue bay.
The bookworms writhe
From rusty musty walls.
They drown themselves like rabbits in the sea.

Venomous foreigners harry mandarins
With pitchfork, blunderbuss and snickersnee.

In the book-slums there is thunder;
Gunpowder, that sad wonder,
Intoxicates the knights and beggar-men.
The old grotesques of war begin again:
Rebels, devils, fairies are set free.

So . . .
Confucius hears a carol and a hum:
A picture sea-child whirs from off his fan
In one quick breath of peach-bloom fantasy.
Then, in an instant bows the reverent knee—
A full-grown sweetheart, chanting his renown.
And then she darts into the Yellow Sea,
Calling, calling:
"Sage with holy brow,
Say farewell to China now;
Live like the swine,
Leave off your scholar-gown!
This city of books is falling, falling,
The Empire of China is crumbling down."

II

Confucius, Confucius, how great was Confucius—
The sage of Shantung, and the master of Mencius?

Alexander fights the East.
Just as the Indus turns him back
He hears of tempting lands beyond,
With sword-swept cities on the rack
With crowns outshining India's crown:
The Empire of China, crumbling down.
Later the Roman sibyls say:
"Egypt, Persia and Macedon,

164

Tyre and Carthage, passed away:
And the Empire of China is crumbling down.
Rome will never crumble down."

III

See how the generations pass—
Like sand through Heaven's blue hour-glass.

Arthur waits on the British shore
One thankful day,
For Galahad sails back at last
To Camelot Bay.

The *pure* knight lands and tells the tale:
"Far in the east
A sea-girl led us to a king,
The king to a feast,
In a land where poppies bloom for miles,
Where books are made like bricks and tiles.
I taught that king to love your name—
Brother and Christian he became.

"His Town of Thunder-Powder keeps
A giant hound that never sleeps,
A crocodile that sits and weeps.

"His Town of Cheese the mouse affrights
With fire-winged cats that light the nights.
They glorify the land of rust;
Their sneeze is music in the dust.
(And deep and ancient is the dust.)

"All towns have one same miracle
With the Town of Silk, the capital—
Vast bookworms in the book-built walls.
Their creeping shakes the silver halls;

They look like cables, and they seem
Like writhing roots on trees of dream.
Their sticky cobwebs cross the street,
Catching scholars by the feet,
Who own the tribes, yet rule them not,
Bitten by bookworms till they rot.
Beggars and clowns rebel in might
Bitten by bookworms till they fight."

Arthur calls to his knights in rows:
"I will go if Merlin goes;
These rebels must be flayed and sliced,
Let us cut their throats for Christ."
But Merlin whispers in his beard:
"China has witches to be feared."
Arthur stares at the sea-foam's rim
Amazed. The fan-girl beckons him!—
That slender and peculiar child
Mongolian and brown and wild.
His eyes grow wide, his senses drown,
She laughs in her wing, like the sleeve of a gown.
She lifts a key of crimson stone.
"The Great Gunpowder-town you own."
She lifts a key with chains and rings:
"I give the town where cats have wings."
She lifts a key as white as milk:
"This unlocks the Town of Silk"—
Throws forty keys at Arthur's feet:
"These unlock the land complete."

Then, frightened by suspicious knights,
And Merlin's eyes like altar-lights,
And the Christian towers of Arthur's town,
She spreads blue fins—she whirs away;
Fleeing far across the bay,
Wailing through the gorgeous day:
"My sick king begs

That you save his crown
And his learned chiefs from the worm and clown—
The Empire of China is crumbling down."

IV

Always the generations pass,
Like sand through Heaven's blue hour-glass!

The time the King of Rome is born—
Napoleon's son, that eaglet thing—
Bonaparte finds beside his throne
One evening, laughing in her wing,
The Chinese sea-child; and she cries,
Breaking his heart with emerald eyes
And fairy-bred unearthly grace:
"Master, take your destined place—
Across white foam and water blue
The streets of China call to you:
The Empire of China is crumbling down."
Then he bends to kiss her mouth,
And gets but incense, dust and drouth.

Custodians, custodians!
Mongols and Manchurians!
Christians, wolves, Mohammedans!

In hard Berlin they cried: "O King,
China's way is a shameful thing!"

In Tokio they cry: "O King,
China's way is a shameful thing!"

And thus our song might call the roll
Of every land from pole to pole,
And every rumor known to time
Of China doddering—or sublime.

V

Slowly the generations pass—
Like sand through Heaven's blue hour-glass.

So let us find tomorrow now:
Our towns are gone;
Our books have passed; ten thousand years
Have thundered on.
The Sphinx looks far across the world
In fury black:
She sees all western nations spent
Or on the rack.
Eastward she sees one land she knew
When from the stone
Priests of the sunrise carved her out
And left her lone.
She sees the shore Confucius walked
On his sorrowful day:
Impudent foreigners rioting,
In the ancient way;
Officials, futile as of old,
Have gowns more bright;
Bookworms are fiercer than of old,
Their skins more white;
Dust is deeper than of old,
More bats are flying;
More songs are written than of old—
More songs are dying.

Where Galahad found forty towns
Now fade and glare
Ten thousand towns with book-tiled roof
And garden-stair,
Where beggars' babies come like showers
Of classic words:
They rule the world—immortal brooks
And magic birds.

The lion Sphinx roars at the sun.
"I hate this nursing you have done!
The meek inherit the earth too long—
When will the world belong to the strong?"
She soars; she claws his patient face—
The girl-moon screams at the disgrace.
The sun's blood fills the western sky;
He hurries not, and will not die.

The baffled Sphinx, on granite wings,
Turns now to where young China sings.
One thousand of ten thousand towns
Go down before her silent wrath;
Yet even lion-gods may faint
And die upon their brilliant path.
She sees the Chinese children romp
In dust that she must breathe and eat.
Her tongue is reddened by its lye;
She craves its grit, its cold and heat.
The Dust of Ages holds a glint
Of fire from the foundation-stones,
Of spangles from the sun's bright face,
Of sapphires from earth's marrow-bones.
Mad-drunk with it, she ends her day—
Slips when a high sea-wall gives way,
Drowns in the cold Confucian sea
Where the whirring fan-girl first flew free.

In the light of the maxims of Chesterfield, Mencius,
Wilson, Roosevelt, Tolstoy, Trotsky,
Franklin or Nietzsche, how great was Confucius?

"*Laughing Asia*" brown and wild,
That lyric and immortal child,
His fan's gay daughter, crowned with sand,
Between the water and the land
Now cries on high in irony,
With a voice of night-wind alchemy:

169

"O cat, O Sphinx,
O stony-face,
The joke is on Egyptian pride,
The joke is on the human race:
'The meek inherit the earth too long—
When will the world belong to the strong?'
I am born from off the holy fan
Of the world's most patient gentleman.
So answer me,
O courteous sea!
O deathless sea!"

And thus will the answering Ocean call:
China will fall,
The Empire of China will crumble down,
When the Alps and the Andes crumble down;
When the sun and the moon have crumbled down,
The Empire of China will crumble down,
Crumble down."

❧ *Section Five*

SONGS, PRAYERS, &

SUPPLICATIONS

TO THE MUSE

🌿 *THE FLOWER-FED BUFFALOES*

The flower-fed buffaloes of the spring
In the days of long ago,
Ranged where the locomotives sing
And the prairie flowers lie low:—
The tossing, blooming, perfumed grass
Is swept away by the wheat,
Wheels and wheels and wheels spin by
In the spring that still is sweet.
But the flower-fed buffaloes of the spring
Left us, long ago.
They gore no more, they bellow no more,
They trundle around the hills no more:—
With the Blackfeet, lying low,
With the Pawnees, lying low,
Lying low.

Last night at black midnight I woke with a cry,
The windows were shaking, there was thunder on high,
The floor was atremble, the door was ajar,
White fires, crimson fires, shone from afar.
I rushed to the dooryard. The city was gone.
My home was a hut without orchard or lawn.
It was mud-smear and logs near a whispering stream,
Nothing else built by man could I see in my dream . . .
Then . . .
Ghost-kings came headlong, row upon row,
Gods of the Indians, torches aglow.

They mounted the bear and the elk and the deer,
And eagles gigantic, aged and sere,
They rode long-horn cattle, they cried "A-la-la."
They lifted the knife, the bow, and the spear,
They lifted ghost-torches from dead fires below,
The midnight made grand with the cry "A-la-la."
The midnight made grand with a red-god charge,
A red-god show,
A red-god show,
"A-la-la, a-la-la, a-la-la, a-la-la."

With bodies like bronze, and terrible eyes
Came the rank and the file, with catamount cries,
Gibbering, yipping, with hollow-skull clacks,
Riding white bronchos with skeleton backs,
Scalp-hunters, beaded and spangled and bad,
Naked and lustful and foaming and mad,
Flashing primeval demoniac scorn,
Blood-thirst and pomp amid darkness reborn,
Power and glory that sleep in the grass
While the winds and the snows and the great rains pass.

*1*74

They crossed the gray river, thousands abreast,
They rode in infinite lines to the west,
Tide upon tide of strange fury and foam,
Spirits and wraiths, the blue was their home,
The sky was their goal where the star-flags were furled,
And on past those far golden splendors they whirled.
They burned to dim meteors, lost in the deep.
And I turned in dazed wonder, thinking of sleep.

And the wind crept by
Alone, unkempt, unsatisfied,
The wind cried and cried—
Muttered of massacres long past,
Buffaloes in shambles vast . . .
An owl said: "Hark, what is a-wing?"
I heard a cricket carolling,
I heard a cricket carolling,
I heard a cricket carolling.

Then . . .
Snuffing the lightning that crashed from on high
Rose royal old buffaloes, row upon row.
The lords of the prairie came galloping by.
And I cried in my heart "A-la-la, a-la-la,
A red-god show,
A red-god show,
A-la-la, a-la-la, a-la-la, a-la-la."

Buffaloes, buffaloes, thousands abreast,
A scourge and amazement, they swept to the west.
With black bobbing noses, with red rolling tongues,
Coughing forth steam from their leather-wrapped lungs,
Cows with their calves, bulls big and vain,
Goring the laggards, shaking the mane,
Stamping flint feet, flashing moon eyes.
Pompous and owlish, shaggy and wise.
Like sea-cliffs and caves resounded their ranks
With shoulders like waves, and undulant flanks.

Tide upon tide of strange fury and foam,
Spirits and wraiths, the blue was their home,
The sky was their goal where the star-flags are furled,
And on past those far golden splendors they whirled.
They burned to dim meteors, lost in the deep,
And I turned in dazed wonder, thinking of sleep.

I heard a cricket's cymbals play,
A scarecrow lightly flapped his rags,
And a pan that hung by his shoulder rang,
Rattled and thumped in a listless way,
And now the wind in the chimney sang,
The wind in the chimney,
The wind in the chimney,
The wind in the chimney,
    Seemed to say:—
"Dream, boy, dream,
If you anywise can.
To dream is the work
Of beast or man.
Life is the west-going dream-storms' breath,
Life is a dream, the sigh of the skies,
The breath of the stars, that nod on their pillows
With their golden hair mussed over their eyes."
The locust played on his musical wing,
Sang to his mate of love's delight.
I heard the whippoorwill's soft fret.
I heard a cricket carolling,
I heard a cricket carolling,
I heard a cricket say: "Good-night, good-night,
Good-night, good-night, . . . good-night."

       .   .   .

❧ JOHNNY APPLESEED'S HYMN
TO THE SUN

Christ the dew in the clod,
    Christ the sap of the trees,
Christ the light in the waterfall,
    Christ the soul of the sun,
Innermost blood of the sun,
    Grant I may touch the fringes
Of the outermost robe of the sun;
    Let me store your rays till my ribs
Carry the breath of lightning,
    Till my lips speak the fullness of thunder
To waken world-weary men:
    Till my whisper engenders lions
Out of the desert weeds.

Give me your eyes, O sun,
    To watch through the universe
Where other suns speed on,
    Brothers, children of God,
Making the great deeps fair.

Take me unto yourself.
    My flesh is a sacrifice,
If only my soul may go
    As a flame to the edge of the sky
Where the sin-born stars come forth
    From the black strong chaos-sea,
From the infinite widths of night.

Grant I may die in a star
    As the chosen of God all die
Rising again in the dreams

Of sinning, star born men,
Destroying their sins forever.

Give me your hidden wings,
    That I may go to the heights
Of the gold-built cliffs of heaven,
    Where jungles in silence reign.
Where the streets, knee-deep in moss
    And the mansions heavy with trees
With Cedars of Lebanon
    With olive and orange and palm
Are silent but for the wind,
    Empty, mysterious.

Give me your strength, O sun!
    Give me your hidden wings,
Till I climb to the holiest place,
    That highest plain of all,
With its glassy shallow pools,
    That desert of level fear
Where three great thrones stand high
    Hewn from three ancient mountains,
Blind thrones of a fair lost land.
    You have left your thrones for the suns,
Great God, O Trinity,
    With all your marvelous hosts,
Cherubim, seraphim.
    You blaze in our eyes by day.
They gleam from the stars by night.

Give us your life, O sun!
    Body and blood of Christ,
Wafer of awful fire
    Give us the contrite heart,
Take out the death from us.

Either the dead are dead,
    Or to-day is eternity,

Your face is eternity,
    Your rays are our endless life.
You are girt with a golden girdle,
    You are with all your crucified
Angels and saints and men
    Who die under clouds in the stars:
You are bringing them back from the dead.
    They breathe on my face as I pray.

Give me your innermost life.
    Come quickly, Alpha, Omega,
Our God, the beginning and end!

❦ JOHNNY APPLESEED'S SHIP
COMES IN

This is the night my ship comes in.
The wine comes pouring down.
Glory and pain! The Angel's blood
Anoints the teeming town.
And the mighty flagship sways and dips,
And I thank my God with fevered lips.
My prophet brings a thousand ships
And the dream of a thorny crown.
He will lead these empty ships like sheep,
He will sail the hills of air,
He will find bold sailors, young as I
Who will love the scars of care—
The care that comes with crimson hands,
From pouring of the wine;
The wine of angels crucified,
The wine of demons crucified,
Brothers of Christ, all crucified
In the stars, and made divine.

We will lead our fleets through newborn skies,
We will scour each rebel world—
Till every lonely deck shall see
Strange prophet-scrolls uncurled
Till every lonely mast shall see
Strange prophet flags unfurled—
Till cataracts from the cups of God
Upon the stars are whirled.

JOHNNY APPLESEED'S WIFE

FROM THE PALACE OF EVE

(*See* Harper's Monthly Magazine *for November, 1871*)

The crickets call through the long, long night
    And the clouds are gray and the wind goes down,
And I wonder and wait in the moonlight white
    For the maid from the Chaos Town. . . .

For the maid from the Palace of Eve to come,
    Soul of my body, blood of my arms,
By love made blind, by fear made dumb,
    A bride, with a bride's alarms:

A girl with the bridal glory red
    From her quivering face to her rosy feet,
With her heaven-made bridal vows all said,
    And mine on earth complete.

O Mother Eve in your deathless power,
    By Adam's throne in the crumbling years,
Send her one murmuring perfect hour
    Of fear and passionate tears!

Let her love be wild as a cataract,
    The storm you knew when the morning came;
Or ever you felt the drouth of noon
    Or the drouth of sin or the drouth of shame.

Make her of bread from out of your hand,
    Make her of honey from your board,
Make her kiss like the lightning brand
    That shall pierce my soul as a sword:

Her breath of songs from the east and west
 And every fragrant wind that blows;
Her splendid knees from the lily's breast
 Her tender feet from the lips of the rose.

Make her a sacrificial fire
 Where noble friendship shall be slain
On the spice-flamed wood of dread desire,
 Stronger in glory and joy and pain.

Make her blood of the grapes of delight,
 A cup of your shadowy garden-wine;
Her breasts of the asphodel so white,
 Her face of the amaranth divine!

 .   .   .

The crickets call through the long, long night,
 And the clouds are gray and the wind goes down,
And I wonder and wait in the moonlight white
 For the maid from the Chaos Town:

From the Chaos Town in the furthest East
 Beyond the edge of the things that are,
Built from the broken rock and mist
 Of many a dead titanic star.

And the hours go on and on and on
 And my empty arms are iron and lead,
And the skies are blue, for the dawn has gone,
 And I wait by a weary bed.

❧ THE FAIRY FROM THE APPLE-SEED

O apple-seed I planted in a silly shallow place
In a bowl of wrought silver, with Sangamon earth within it,
O baby tree that came, without an apple on it,
A tree that grew a tiny height, but thickened an apace,
With bossy glossy arms, and leaves of trembling lace.

One night the trunk was rent, and the heavy bowl rocked
     round,
The boughs were bending here and there, with a curious
     locust sound,
And a tiny dryad came, from out the doll tree,
And held the boughs in ivory hands,
And waved her black hair round,
And climbed, and ate with merry words
The sudden fruit it bore.
And in the leaves she hides and sings
And guards my study door.

She guards it like a watchdog true
And robbers run away.
Her eyes are lifted spears all night,
But dove-eyes in the day.

And she is stranger, stronger
Than the funny human race.
Lovelier her form, and holier her face.
She feeds me flowers and fruit
With a quaint grace.
She dresses in the apple-leaves
As delicate as lace.
This girl that came from Sangamon earth
In a bowl of silver bright
From an apple-seed I planted in a silly shallow place.

183

❧ THE SEA SERPENT CHANTEY

I

There's a snake on the western wave
And his crest is red.
He is long as a city street,
And he eats the dead.
There's a hole in the bottom of the sea
Where the snake goes down.
And he waits in the bottom of the sea
For the men that drown.
            Chorus:—

Let the audi-
ence join in
the chorus.

This is the voice of the sand
(The sailors understand)
"There is far more sea than sand,
There is far more sea than land.
            Yo . . . ho, yo . . . ho."

II

He waits by the door of his cave
While the ages moan.
He cracks the ribs of the ships
With his teeth of stone.
In his gizzard deep and long
Much treasure lies.
Oh, the pearls and the Spanish gold. . . .
And the idols' eyes. . . .
Oh, the totem poles . . . the skulls . . .
The altars cold . . .
The wedding rings, the dice . . .
The buoy bells old.
            Chorus:—This is the voice, etc.

III

Dive, mermaids, with sharp swords
And cut him through,
And bring us the idols' eyes
And the red gold too.
Lower the grappling hooks
Good pirate men
And drag him up by the tongue
From his deep wet den.
We will sail to the end of the world,
We will nail his hide
To the mainmast of the moon
In the evening tide.

*Repeat as a
second chorus
many times.*

IV

Or will you let him live,
The deep-sea thing,
With the wrecks of all the world
In a black wide ring
By the hole in the bottom of the sea
Where the snake goes down,
Where he waits in the bottom of the sea
For the men that drown?
    Chorus:—This is the voice, etc.

❧ THE LAME BOY AND THE FAIRY

(*To the rhythm of Chopin's "Berceuse"*)

A lame boy
Met a fairy
In a meadow
Where the bells grow.

And the fairy
Kissed him gaily.

And the fairy
Gave him friendship,
Gave him healing,
Gave him wings.

"All the fashions
I will give you.
You will fly, dear,
All the long year.

"Wings of springtime,
Wings of summer,
Wings of autumn,
Wings of winter!

"Here is
A dress for springtime."
And she gave him
A dress of grasses,
Orchard blossoms,
Wild-flowers found in
Mountain passes,
*Shoes of song and
Wings of rhyme.*

"Here is
A dress for summer."
And she gave him
A hat of sunflowers,
A suit of poppies,
Clover, daisies,
All from wheat-sheaves
In harvest time;
*Shoes of song and
Wings of rhyme.*

"Here is
A dress for autumn."
And she gave him
A suit of red haw,
Hickory, apple,
Elder, pawpaw,
Maple, hazel,
Elm and grape leaves,
And blue
And white
Cloaks of smoke,
And veils of sunlight,
From the Indian summer prime!
*Shoes of song and
Wings of rhyme.*

"Here is
A dress for winter."
And she gave him
A polar bear suit,
And he heard the
Christmas horns toot,
And she gave him
Green festoons and
Red balloons and
All the sweet cakes
And the snowflakes

187

Of Christmas time,
Shoes of song and
Wings of rhyme.

And the fairy
Kept him laughing,
Led him dancing,
Kept him climbing
On the hilltops
Toward the moon.

"We shall see silver ships.
We shall see singing ships,
Valleys of spray today,
Mountains of foam.
We have been long away,
Far from our wonderland.
Here come the ships of love
Taking us home.

"Who are our captains bold?
They are the saints of old.
One is Saint Christopher.
He takes your hand.
He leads the cloudy fleet.
He gives us bread and meat.
His is our ship till
We reach our dear land.

"Where is our house to be?
Far in the ether sea.
There where the North Star
Is moored in the deep.
Sleepy old comets nod
There on the silver sod.
Sleepy young fairy flowers
Laugh in their sleep.

"A hundred years
And
A day,
There we will fly
And play
I-spy and *cross-tag*.
And meet on the highway,
And call to the game
Little Red Riding Hood,
Goldilocks, Santa Claus,
Every beloved
And heart-shaking name."

And the lame child
And the fairy
Journeyed far, far
To the North Star.

❧ THE DREAM OF ALL THE
SPRINGFIELD WRITERS

I'll haunt this town, though gone the maids and men,
The darling few, my friends and loves to-day.
My ghost returns, bearing a great sword-pen
When far-off children of their children play.

That pen will drip with moonlight and with fire.
I'll write upon the church-doors and the walls.
And reading there, young hearts shall leap the higher
Though drunk already with their own love-calls.

Still led of love and arm in arm, strange gold
Shall find in tracing the far-speeding track
The dauntless war-cries that my sword-pen bold
Shall carve on terraces and tree-trunks black—

On tree-trunks black beneath the blossoms white:—
Just as the phosphorent merman, bound for home
Jewels his fire-path in the tides at night
While hurrying sea-babes follow through the foam.

And in December when the leaves are dead
And the first snow has carpeted the street
While young cheeks flush a healthful Christmas red
And young eyes glisten with youth's fervor sweet—

My pen shall cut in winter's snowy floor
Cries that in channeled glory leap and shine,
My Village Gospel, living evermore
Amid rejoicing, loyal friends of mine.

❦ AN APOLOGY FOR THE
BOTTLE VOLCANIC

Sometimes I dip my pen and find the bottle full of fire,
The salamanders flying forth I cannot but admire.
It's Etna, or Vesuvius, if those big things were small,
And then 'tis but itself again, and does not smoke at all.
And so my blood grows cold. I say, "The bottle held but
ink,
And, if you thought it otherwise, the worser for your
think."
And then, just as I throw my scribbled paper on the floor,
The bottle says, "Fe, fi, fo, fum," and steams and shouts
some more.
O sad, deceiving ink, as bad as liquor in its way—
All demons of a bottle size have pranced from you to-day,
And seized my pen for hobby-horse as witches ride a
broom,
And left a trail of brimstone words and blots and gobs of
gloom.
And yet when I am extra good and say my prayers at night,
And mind my ma, and do the chores, and speak to folks
polite,
My bottle spreads a rainbow-mist, and from the vapor fine
Ten thousand troops from fairyland come riding in a line.
I've seen them on their chargers race around my study chair,
They opened wide the window and rode forth upon the air.
The army widened as it went, and into myriads grew,
O how the lances shimmered, how the silvery trumpets
blew!

❦ THE MOUSE THAT GNAWED
THE OAK-TREE DOWN

The mouse that gnawed the oak-tree down
Began his task in early life.
He kept so busy with his teeth
He had no time to take a wife.

He gnawed and gnawed through sun and rain
When the ambitious fit was on,
Then rested in the sawdust till
A month of idleness had gone.

He did not move about to hunt
The coteries of mousie-men.
He was a snail-paced, stupid thing
Until he cared to gnaw again.

The mouse that gnawed the oak-tree down,
When that tough foe was at his feet—
Found in the stump no angel-cake
Nor buttered bread, nor cheese nor meat—
The forest-roof let in the sky.
"This light is worth the work," said he.
"I'll make this ancient swamp more light,"
And started on another tree.

"Bring me soft song," said Aladdin.
"This tailor-shop sings not at all.
Chant me a word of the twilight,
Of roses that mourn in the fall.
Bring me a song like hashish
That will comfort the stale and the sad,
For I would be mending my spirit,
Forgetting these days that are bad,
Forgetting companions too shallow,
Their quarrels and arguments thin,
Forgetting the shouting Muezzin":
"I AM YOUR SLAVE," said the Jinn.

"Bring me old wines," said Aladdin.
"I have been a starved pauper too long.
Serve them in vessels of jade and of shell,
Serve them with fruit and with song:—
Wines of pre-Adamite Sultans
Digged from beneath the black seas:—
New-gathered dew from the heavens
Dripped down from Heaven's sweet trees,
Cups from the angels' pale tables
That will make me both handsome and wise,
For I have beheld her, the princess,
Firelight and starlight her eyes.
Pauper I am, I would woo her.
And—let me drink wine, to begin,
Though the Koran expressly forbids it."
"I AM YOUR SLAVE," said the Jinn.

"Plan me a dome," said Aladdin,
"That is drawn like the dawn of the MOON,
When the sphere seems to rest on the mountains,

Half-hidden, yet full-risen soon.
Build me a dome," said Aladdin,
"That shall cause all young lovers to sigh,
The fullness of life and of beauty,
Peace beyond peace to the eye—
A palace of foam and of opal,
Pure moonlight without and within,
Where I may enthrone my sweet lady."
"I AM YOUR SLAVE," said the Jinn.

❧ THE TRAMP'S REFUSAL

On Being Asked by a Beautiful Gypsy to Join Her
Group of Strolling Players

Lady, I cannot act, though I admire
God's great chameleons Booth-Barret men.
But when the trees are green, my thoughts may be
October-red. December comes again
And snowy Christmas there within my breast
Though I be walking in the August dust.
Often my lone contrary sword is bright
When every other soldier's sword is rust.
Sometimes, while churchly friends go up to God
On wings of prayer to altars of delight
I walk and talk with Satan, call him friend,
And greet the imps with converse most polite.
When hunger nips me, then at once I knock
At the near farmer's door and ask for bread.
I must, when I have wrought a curious song
Pin down some stranger till the thing is read.
When weeds choke up within, then look to me
To show the world the manners of a weed.
I cannot change my cloak except my heart
Has changed and set the fashion for the deed.
When love betrays me I go forth to tell
The first kind gossip that too-patent fact.
I cannot pose at hunger, love or shame.
It plagues me not to say: "I cannot act."
I only mourn that this unharnessed *me*
Walks with the devil far too much each day.
I would be chained to angel-kings of fire.
And whipped and driven up the heavenly way.

LITANY OF THE HEROES

(Inscribed to George Mather Richards)

Egypt and Israel in History.

Would that young Amenophis Fourth returned
Prince Hamlet and the Poet Keats in one,
He mocked at fraud, even his own crown,
He loved all classic beauty in the town,
He rode abroad to build his lotus tomb,
Praising one god, and that one god, the sun.
The idol-worshippers chipped out his name
From wall and obelisk, to end his fame.

Still let that brave, flower-loving King of Time
Be throned in your deep hearts, to raise for you
The hopes the prince and his mother Thi, well knew,
Filling these barren days with Mystery,
With Life, and Death, and Immorality,
The devouring ages, the triumphant Sun.
God keep us brooding on eternal things,
God make us wizard-kings.

Then let us raise that Egypt-nurtured youth,
Son of a Hebrew, with the dauntless scorn
And hate for bleating gods Egyptian-born,
Showing with signs to stubborn Mizraim
"God is one God, the God of Abraham,"
He who in the beginning *made* the Sun.
God send us Moses from his hidden grave,
God help us to be brave.

The Soul of China in History.

Would we were scholars of Confucius' time
Watching the feudal China crumbling down,
Frightening our master, shaking many a crown,
Until he makes more firm the father sages,

Restoring custom from the earliest ages
With prudent sayings, golden as the sun.
Lord, show us safe, august, established ways,
Fill us with yesterdays.

Would that by Hindu magic we became
Dark monks of jewelled India long ago,
Sitting at Prince Siddartha's feet to know
The foolishness of gold and love and station,
The Gospel of the Great Renunciation,
The ragged cloak, the staff, the rain and sun,
The beggar's life, with far Nirvana gleaming:
Lord, make us Buddhas, dreaming.

*The
Soul of
India
in History.*

Would that the joy of living came to-day,
Even as sculptured on Athena's shrine
In sunny conclave of serene design,
Maidens and men, procession flute and feast,
By Phidias, the ivory-hearted priest
Of beauty absolute, whose eyes the sun
Showed goodlier forms than our desires can guess
And more of happiness.

*The
Classic
Spirit.*

Would I might waken in you Alexander,
Murdering the nations wickedly,
Flooding his time with blood remorselessly,
Sowing new Empires, where the Athenian light,
Knowledge and music, slay the Asian night,
And men behold Apollo in the sun.
God make us splendid, though by grievous wrong.
God make us fierce and strong.

Would I might rouse the Cæsar in you all
(That which men hail as king, and bow them down)
Till you are crowned, or you refuse the crown.
Would I might wake the valor and the pride,
The eagle soul with which he soared and died,

Entering grandly then the fearful grave.
God help us build the world, like master-men,
God help us to be brave.

*Great
Art and
Letters
in
History.*

Behold the Pharisees, proud, rich, and damned,
Boasting themselves in lost Jerusalem,
Gathered a weeping woman to condemn,
Then watching curiously, without a sound
The God of Mercy, writing on the ground.
How looked his sunburned face beneath the sun
Flushed with his Father's mighty angel-wine?
God make us all divine.

Would I might free St. Paul, singing in chains
In your deep hearts. New heavenly love shall fight
And slay the subtle gods of Greek delight
And dreadful Roman gods, and light the world
With words of flame, till those false powers are hurled
Burning to ashes in the avenging grave.
"St. Paul" our battle-cry, and faith our shield,
God help us to be brave.

Yea, give the world no peace, till all men kneel,
Seeking with tears the grace of Christ our God.
Make us like Augustine beneath Thy rod.
Give us no other joy but Thy repentance,
Thunder our just, hereditary sentence
Till shame and fear of Hell blot out the sun.
Christ help us hold Thy blood-redemption dear.
Christ, give us holy fear.

*The
Secular
Spirit
in
History.*

Nay, let us have the marble peace of Rome,
Recorded in the Code Justinian,
Till Pagan Justice shelters man from man.
Fanatics snarl like mongrel dogs; the code
Will build each custom like a Roman Road,
Direct as daylight, clear-eyed as the sun.
God grant all crazy world-disturbers cease.
God give us honest peace.

Would that on horses swifter than desire
We rode behind Mohammed 'round the zones
With swords unceasing, sowing fields of bones,
Till New America, ancient Mizraim,
Cry: "Allah is the God of Abraham."
God make our host relentless as the sun,
Each soul your spear, your banner and your slave,
God help us to be brave.

The World-Spirit of Islam.

Would I might wake St. Francis in you all,
Brother of birds and trees, God's Troubadour,
Blinded with weeping for the sad and poor;
Our wealth undone, all strict Franciscan men,
Come, let us chant the canticle again
Of mother earth and the enduring sun.
God make each soul the lonely leper's slave;
God make us saints, and brave.

The Medieval Spirit in History.

Would we were lean and grim, and shaken with hate
Like Dante, fugitive, o'er-wrought with cares,
And climbing bitterly the stranger's stairs,
Yet Love, Love, Love, divining: finding still
Beyond dark Hell the penitential hill,
And blessed Beatrice beyond the grave.
Jehovah lead us through the wilderness:
God make our wandering brave.

Would that we had the fortunes of Columbus.
Sailing his caravels a trackless way,
He found a Universe—he sought Cathay.
God give such dawns as when, his venture o'er,
The Sailor looked upon San Salvador.
God lead us past the setting of the sun
To wizard islands, of august surprise;
God make our blunders wise.

Would that such hills and cities round us sang,
Such vistas of the actual earth and man
As kindled Titian when his life began;

Religion in History.

199

Would that this latter Greek could put his gold,
Wisdom and splendor in our brushes bold
Till Greece and Venice, children of the sun,
Become our everyday, and we aspire
To colors fairer far, and glories higher.

Would I might wake in you the whirlwind soul
Of Michelangelo, who hewed the stone
And Night and Day revealed, whose arm alone
Could draw the face of God, the titan high
Whose genius smote like lightning from the sky—
And shall he mold like dead leaves in the grave?
Nay, he is in us! Let us dare and dare.
God help us to be brave.

Would that in body and spirit Shakespeare came
Visible emperor of the deeds of Time,
With Justice still the genius of his rhyme,
Giving each man his due, each passion grace,
Impartial as the rain from Heaven's face
Or sunshine from the Heaven-enthroned sun.
Sweet Swan of Avon, come to us again.
Teach us to write, and writing, to be men.

Would we were blind with Milton, and we sang
With him of uttermost Heaven in a new song,
That men might see again the angel-throng,
And newborn hopes, true to this age, would rise,
Pictures to make men weep for paradise,
All glorious things beyond the defeated grave.
God smite us blind, and give us bolder wings;
God help us to be brave.

The
Napoleonic
Ideal
in
History.

Would that the cold adventurous Corsican
Woke with new hope of glory, strong from sleep,
Instructed how to conquer and to keep
More justly, having dreamed awhile, yea crowned

With shining flowers, God-given; while the sound
Of singing continents, following the sun,
Calls freeborn men to guard Napoleon's throne
Who makes the eternal hopes of man his own.

Would that the dry hot wind called Science came, *The Eye*
Forerunner of a higher mystic day, *of*
Though vile machine-made commerce clear the way— *Science*
Though nature losing shame should lose her veil, *in History.*
And ghosts of buried angel-warriors wail
The fall of Heaven, and the relentless Sun
Smile on, as Abraham's God forever dies—
Lord, give us Darwin's eyes!

Would I might rouse the Lincoln in you all, *The*
That which is gendered in the wilderness *American*
From lonely prairies and God's tenderness. *Spirit in*
Imperial soul, star of a weedy stream, *History.*
Born where the ghosts of buffaloes still gleam,
Whose spirit hoof-beats storm above his grave,
Above that breast of earth and prairie-fire—
Fire that freed the slave.

Then let us seek out shining Emerson
Teacher of Whitman, and better priest of man,
The self-reliant granite American.
Give us his Heaven-sent right to strike and spare,
Give us the wools and hair-shirts prophets wear,
Then Adam's freedom in the Eden-sun.
God help us make each state an Eden-flower,
And blaze long trails to power.

These were the spacious days of Roosevelt.
Would that among you chiefs like him arose
To win the wrath of our united foes,
To chain King Mammon in the donjon-keep,
To rouse our godly citizens that sleep
Till, as one soul, we shout up to the sun

The battle-yell of freedom and the right—
"Lord, let good men unite."

Nay, I would have you lonely and despised.
Statesmen whom only statesmen understand,
Artists whom only artists can command,
Sages whom all but sages scorn, whose fame
Dies down in lies, in synonyms for shame
With the best populace beneath the sun.
God gives us tasks that martyrs can revere,
Still too much hated to be whispered here.

*The
Conclusion
and the
Ultimate
and Final
Heroes of
This Song:
Wilson and
Socrates.*

Yea, I would have you like stern Woodrow Wilson
Drinking his cup, as such proud men have done
Since Amenophis Fourth addressed the sun.
Staking his last strength and his final fight
That cost him all, to set the old world right.
The League of Nations course is yet to run.
The Idol-worshippers would end its fame,
And cut from every wall its builder's name.

Would we might drink, with knowledge high and kind,
The hemlock cup of Socrates the king,
Knowing right well we know not anything,
With full life done, bowing before the law,
Binding young thinkers' hearts with loyal awe,
And fealty fixed as the ever-enduring sun—
God let us live, seeking the highest light,
God help us die aright.

Nay, I would have you grand, and still forgotten,
Hid like the stars at noon, as he who set
The Egyptian magic of man's alphabet;
Or that Egyptian, first to dream in pain
That dauntless souls cannot by death be slain—
Conquering for all men then, the fearful grave.
God keep us hid, yet vaster far than death.
God help us to be brave.

❦ BABYLON, BABYLON,
BABYLON THE GREAT

(Inscribed to Carl Sandburg)

This poem is based on the episode of "Lincoln's Lost Speech," too dangerous to print at the time, at Cooper Union, his first appearance in the East.

Isaiah, the country-boy, marched against the jazz—
Babylon the shrewd and slick, Babylon the great.
Jeremiah, Ezekiel, Daniel, walked alone,
Alone against Babylon, alone against fate.
St. Paul walked alone, St. Peter walked alone,
Against that town to marvel on, Babylon the great.

Lincoln at Cooper Union, improvised and chanted,
Threw away his speech, and told tales out of school,
Changed from politician to God's divine fool.
Beside himself, beyond himself, set his old heart free,
The flame spread, the flame spread, every suppressed word
   was said,
Isaiah's voice from the dead;
Lincoln's great lost speech, nowhere written down,
But it burned every gate of the famous old town.

Lincoln at Cooper Union, called down fire from Heaven,
Overthrew jazz—Babylon, Babylon the great.

I have seen the burning of Babylon's gardens,
Many and many a noble day.
I have watched the ashes of that beautiful lost city,
Blown through many a year away.

Statesmen have torn down Babylon. . . . The gophers have
   buried Babylon. . . .

Coyotes lope through Babylon. . . . Prairie dogs bore the
clay and sand. . . .
Texas cattle have trampled Babylon deeper in dung and
dust. . . .
But forever stands Babylon, fresh in the sunrise, . . .
Foam upon the ocean . . . or granite on the land,
As new as the Devil, and the Devil's lust.

How our tales of Babylon multiply upon the ranges!
How old memories of victory renew!
Except for the warfare of the youngsters against Babylon,
The campfire songs would be few.

Troubadour!—March with bleeding feet against Babylon!—
(So, keep going to the sun! So, keep going to the sun!)
—If you would be a man.—As these have done before!
As lonely as Lincoln, dazed in Babylon,
Plod, plod, with a heartache, through the Devil's own door!
Tear up your set speeches, improvise once more!

War must begin against that city's music,
So—sing a silly song. Say:—"The sky is blue."
Sing a song of rainbow gems, unknown to Babylon.
Then improvise a song of the mick who lifts the hod,
Of the mick who sets in concrete the steel truss and rod,
Who builds the auto highways across the prairie sod—
(So, keep going to the sun! So, keep going to the sun!)
Improvise a cowboy song, of cactus and of dew,
And of raging on a mustang across the alkali
To where the snow-bright mountains of new mediation lie,
To the Indian basket-flowers, the ferns, the meadow-rue;
Sing of beans in the pod, and of wheat in the shock,
Of hay in the stack, and windmills in the air,
Of castellated silos, and turkeys fat and fair,
Of chickens and of guineas, of pheasants, quails and eagles,
Of the High-School senior boys, foot-ball players, Sheiks
and swells,
Of Lincoln-highway roses and sweet lovers everywhere:—

And the candies and the vanities of senior High-School
    belles,
(So, keep going to the sun! So, keep going to the sun!)

Sing a Kansas love-song, modest, clean and true.
Sing a Kansas love-song, modest, clean and true.
Then lift your psalm of the Manna of our God!
It is the only way to go into Babylon,
Call down fire from Heaven, and the world renew.

This is the only way a bard is a man.
So lift your proud word against the towers if you can.
Go on, with your guitar, through the Devil's breezy gate.
March on, with simple Lincoln against Babylon, Babylon,—
His dog-eared carpet-bag crammed with state papers,
His sweaty old duster flapping like a rag.—
Go, with prairie Lincoln against Babylon, Babylon,
Go with that tall prophet, again to Cooper Union.
March with mighty Lincoln against Babylon the Great!
(So—keep going to the sun! So—keep going to the sun!)

In this poem I have exhorted Sandburg to improvise, but in a
way the opposite of jazz—for I have always hated jazz, as our most
Babylonian disease. This poem originally appeared in Christopher
Morley's Bowling Green column, in *The New York Evening Post*,
to celebrate a visit of Carl Sandburg to New York City. Several
months later it was printed in Memphis, Tennessee, by the author,
in anticipation of Carl Sandburg's visit to address Memphis in a
recital for the Goodwyn Institute, November 17, 1923. I issued it in
a three-foot broadside, with my picture of Babylon at the top as a
kind of hieroglyphic. It was distributed through the kindness of Mrs.
Dicken's Book-Shop.

❧ I KNOW ALL THIS WHEN
GIPSY FIDDLES CRY

Oh, gipsies, proud and stiff-necked and perverse,
Saying: "We tell the fortunes of the nations,
And revel in the deep palm of the world.
The head-line is the road we choose for trade.
The love-line is the lane wherein we camp.
The life-line is the road we wander on.
Mount Venus, Jupiter, and all the rest
Are finger-tips of ranges clasping round
And holding up the Romany's wide sky."
Oh, gipsies, proud and stiff-necked and perverse,
Saying: "We will swap horses till the doom,
And mend the pots and kettles of mankind,
And lend our sons to big-time vaudeville,
Or to the race-track, or the learned world.
But India's Brahma waits within their breasts.
They will return to us with gipsy grins,
And chatter Romany, and shake their curls
And hug the dirtiest babies in the camp.
They will return to the moving pillar of smoke,
The whitest toothed, the merriest laughers known,
The blackest haired of all the tribes of men.
What trap can hold such cats? The Romany
Has crossed such delicate palms with lead or gold,
Wheedling in sun and rain, through perilous years,
All coins now look alike. The palm is all.
Our greasy pack of cards is still the book
Most read of men. The heart's librarians,
We tell all lovers what they want to know.
So, out of the famed Chicago Library,
Out of the great Chicago orchestras,
Out of the skyscraper, the Fine Arts Building,

Our sons will come with fiddles and with loot,
Dressed, as of old, like turkey-cocks and zebras,
Like tiger-lilies and chameleons,
Go west with us to California,
Telling the fortunes of the bleeding world,
And kiss the sunset, ere their day is done."
Oh, gipsies, proud and stiff-necked and perverse
Picking the brains and pockets of mankind,
You will go westward for one-half hour yet.
You will turn eastward in a little while.
You will go back, as men turn to Kentucky,
Land of their fathers, dark and bloody ground.
When all the Jews go home to Syria,
When Chinese cooks go back to Canton, China,
When Japanese photographers return
With their black cameras to Tokio,
And Irish patriots to Donegal,
And Scotch accountants back to Edinburgh,
You will go back to India, whence you came.
When you have reached the borders of your quest,
Homesick at last, by many a devious way,
Winding the wonderlands circuitous,
By foot and horse will trace the long way back!
Fiddling for ocean liners, while the dance
Sweeps through the decks, your brown tribes all will go!
Those east-bound ships will hear your long farewell
On fiddle, piccolo, and flute and timbrel.
I know all this, when gipsy fiddles cry.

That hour of their homesickness, I myself
Will turn, will say farewell to Illinois,
To old Kentucky and Virginia,
And go with them to India, whence they came.
For they have heard a singing from the Ganges,
And cries of orioles,—from the temple caves,—
And Bengal's oldest, humblest villages.
They smell the supper smokes of Amritsar.
Green monkeys cry in Sanskrit to their souls

From lofty bamboo trees of hot Madras.
They think of towns to ease their feverish eyes,
And make them stand and meditate forever,
Domes of astonishment, to heal the mind.
I know all this, when gipsy fiddles cry.

What music will be blended with the wind
When gipsy fiddlers, nearing that old land,
Bring tunes from all the world to Brahma's house?
Passing the Indus, winding poisonous forests,
Blowing soft flutes at scandalous temple girls,
Filling the highways with their magpie loot,
What brass from my Chicago will they heap,
What gems from Walla Walla, Omaha,
Will they pile near the Bodhi Tree, and laugh?
They will dance near such temples as best suit them,
Though they will not quite enter, or adore,
Looking on roofs, as poets look on lilies,
Looking at towers, as boys at forest vines,
That leap to tree-tops through the dizzy air.
I know all this, when gipsy fiddles cry.

And with the gipsies there will be a king
And a thousand desperadoes just his style,
With all their rags dyed in the blood of roses,
Splashed with the blood of angels, and of demons.
And he will boss them with an awful voice.
And with a red whip he will beat his wife.
He will be wicked on that sacred shore,
And rattle cruel spurs against the rocks,
And shake Calcutta's walls with circus bugles.
He will kill Brahmins there, in Kali's name,
And please the thugs, and blood-drunk of the earth.
I know all this, when gipsy fiddles cry.

Oh, sweating thieves, and hard-boiled scalawags,
That still will boast your pride until the doom.
Smashing every caste rule of the world,

Reaching at last your Hindu goal to smash
The caste rules of old India, and shout:
"Down with the Brahmins, let the Romany reign."

When gipsy girls look deep within my hand
They always speak so tenderly and say
That I am one of those star-crossed to wed
A princess in a forest fairy-tale.
So there will be a tender gipsy princess,
My Juliet, shining through this clan.
And I would sing you of her beauty now.
And I will fight with knives the gipsy man
Who tries to steal her wild young heart away.
And I will kiss her in the waterfalls,
And at the rainbow's end, and in the incense
That curls about the feet of sleeping gods,
And sing with her in canebrakes and in rice fields,
In Romany, eternal Romany.
We will sow secret herbs, and plant old roses,
And fumble through dark, snaky palaces,
Stable our ponies in the Taj Mahal,
And sleep outdoors ourselves.
In her strange fairy mill-wheel eyes will wait
All windings and unwindings of the highways,
From India, across America,—
All windings and unwindings of my fancy,
All windings and unwindings of all souls,
All windings and unwindings of the heavens.
I know all this, when gipsy fiddles cry.

We gipsies, proud and stiff-necked and perverse,
Standing upon the white Himalayas,
Will think of far divine Yosemite.
We will heal Hindu hermits there with oil
Brought from California's tall sequoias.
And we will be like gods that heap the thunders,
And start young redwood trees on Time's own mountains,
We will swap horses with the rising moon,

And mend that funny skillet called Orion,
Color the stars like San Francisco's street-lights,
And paint our sign and signature on high
In planets like a bed of crimson pansies;
While a million fiddles shake all listening hearts,
Crying good fortune to the Universe,
Whispering adventure to the Ganges waves,
And to the spirits, and all winds and gods.
Till mighty Brahma puts his golden palm
Within the gipsy king's great striped tent,
And asks his fortune told by that great love-line
That winds across his palm in splendid flame.

Only the hearthstone of old India
Will end the endless march of gipsy feet.
I will go back to India with them
When they go back to India whence they came.
I know all this, when gipsy fiddles cry.